Software Testing

ISEB Intermediate
Certificate

D1396134

The British Computer Society

BCS is the leading professional body for the IT industry. With members in over 100 countries, BCS is the professional and learned Society in the field of computers and information systems.

BCS is responsible for setting standards for the IT profession. It is also leading the change in public perception and appreciation of the economic and social importance of professionally managed IT projects and programmes. In this capacity, the society advises, informs and persuades industry and government on successful IT implementation.

IT is affecting every part of our lives and that is why BCS is determined to promote IT as the profession of the 21st century.

Joining BCS

BCS qualifications, products and services are designed with your career plans in mind. We not only provide essential recognition through professional qualifications but also offer many other useful benefits to our members at every level.

BCS Membership demonstrates your commitment to professional development. It helps to set you apart from other IT practitioners and provides industry recognition of your skills and experience. Employers and customers increasingly require proof of professional qualifications and competence. Professional membership confirms your competence and integrity and sets an independent standard that people can trust. Professional Membership (MBCS) is the pathway to Chartered IT Professional (CITP) Status.

www.bcs.org/membership

Further Information

Further information about BCS can be obtained from: BCS, First Floor, Block D, North Star House, North Star Avenue, Swindon SN2 1FA, UK.

www.bcs.org/contact

Software Testing

An ISEB Intermediate Certificate

Brian Hambling

Angelina Samaroo

Published by British Informatics Society Limited (BISL), a wholly owened subsidiary of BCS, First Floor, Block D, North Star House, North Star Avenue, Swindon, SN2 1FA, UK.

www.bcs.org

ISBN 978-1-906124-13-7

British Cataloguing in Publication Data.
A CIP catalogue record for this book is available at the British Library.

Disclaimer:
The views expressed in this book are those of the authors and do not necessarily reflect the views of BISL or BCS except where explicitly stated as such.
Although every care has been taken by the authors and BISL in the preparation of the publication, no warranty is given by the authors or BISL as publisher as to the accuracy or completeness of the information contained within it and neither the authors nor BISL shall be responsible or liable for any loss or damage whatsoever arising by virtue of such information or any instructions or advice contained within this publication or by any of the aforementioned.

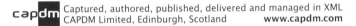 Captured, authored, published, delivered and managed in XML
CAPDM Limited, Edinburgh, Scotland   www.capdm.com

Printed by CPI Antony Rowe Ltd, Chippenham, UK

Contents

Figures and tables

Authors

Brian Hambling has been a software professional for over 30 years. His initial experience in real-time software development in the RAF led to a period in project management for radar simulation development with Marconi Radar Systems. From there he went to Thames Polytechnic (now the University of Greenwich) as Head of the Systems and Software Engineering teaching group for three years before starting a career as an independent consultant. It was at this stage in his career that he became more involved with testing and the broader discipline of quality management. As a Lead TickIT Auditor Brian gained experience of how quality management systems are implemented, and he also became involved in training TickIT auditors, both for their initial qualification and at a more advanced level for their continuing development. In 1997 he accepted the challenge of training testing professionals for deployment as testing consultants for ImagoQA, and as a result of his success in that role, he became ImagoQA's Technical Director in 1998. He continued in that role until ImagoQA was acquired by Microgen UK plc, and he stayed with Microgen to integrate the testing business into their broader IT services portfolio. Since leaving Microgen at the end of 2004 Brian has concentrated on his work in two related areas: for ISEB he has taken on the role of Chief Examiner for software testing qualifications; for the Open University he has continued in the distance teaching role that has occupied much of his spare time for nearly 20 years. More recently he has become increasingly involved in course development for the postgraduate programmes in Computing and Technology, the promotion of Open University courses overseas through OU Worldwide and managing a consultancy programme with a major multinational company.

Angelina Samaroo started her career in the Defence sector, working on the Tornado ADV, where she was exposed to all aspects of the software development life cycle. In 1995 she was awarded Chartered Engineer status by the Royal Aeronautical Society.

Early in her career she took an interest in developing staff, beginning with training new engineers in the testing team, then moving to managing the training of new engineers across the company, to the standards laid down by the IEE (now the IET).

In 1999 she joined the commercial sector, and once again became involved in staff development. She became an instructor for the ISEB Foundation Course in Software Testing and then managed the business unit dealing with training of both internal consultants and external clients. Her team developed the first course to be accredited by ISEB, for the Practitioner Certificate in Software Testing, early in 2002.

Angelina has also instructed delegates in other aspects of testing, such as unit testing, user acceptance testing and managing testing projects, in the UK, Europe, America and Australia.

She currently works for Pinta Education Limited.

Acknowledgements

The authors acknowledge the significant efforts of Matthew Flynn, Suzanne Peart and Rachael Kavanagh of the BCS and ISEB in bringing this book to fruition and making the qualification a worldwide success.

Preface

The book covers the Intermediate certificate syllabus, explaining what the syllabus means and what needs to be known and understood for the examination. Each chapter relates to one section of the syllabus and includes self-diagnostic questions to provide the reader with a quick guide to how much preparation they might need for that section. Each chapter ends with sample questions in the style of the Intermediate examination. Guidance is given on how to prepare for the examination and on examination technique.

Introduction

ISEB SOFTWARE TESTING CERTIFICATES

The Information Systems Examination Board (ISEB) of the British Computer Society awards qualifications in a very broad range of subject areas, of which software testing is one of the most popular. Software testing currently has three levels of certification: Foundation, Intermediate and Practitioner.

The ISEB Foundation Certificate was first offered in 1998 and became an immediate success. It was followed in 2002 by a Software Testing Practitioner Certificate. Demand for the Practitioner Certificate was initially lower than that for the Foundation certificate for a variety of reasons: not every Foundation holder would wish to proceed to the much more advanced Practitioner level qualification, especially if they were not professional testers; many employers, at the time, did not feel the need for more than a very few testers with the more advanced qualification; most significant of all, many of those who wished to proceed to Practitioner found the transition particularly challenging.

The updating of the Foundation syllabus in 2005 inevitably created some inconsistencies between the new Foundation syllabus and the older Practitioner syllabus, and this situation served to emphasise the need for an update to the Practitioner syllabus. As a result, in 2007 ISEB decided to update the Practitioner syllabus, taking the opportunity to make some other changes, of which three were particularly significant:

- The Practitioner syllabus was split into two separate syllabuses to cover each of the two main Software Testing Practitioner disciplines: test management and test analysis.
- The new Practitioner syllabuses were structured around objective measures of required levels of understanding (K levels, which are introduced on page 3 and explained in Appendix B).
- Some changes were made to reflect new topics introduced at Foundation and to bring the Practitioner syllabuses more in line with the state of testing in 2007.

These were necessary changes but they could not solve the problem of the distance between the Foundation and the Practitioner levels of qualification. So one further change was recognised as necessary to make the transition from the Foundation to the Practitioner level more achievable and more attractive. This important change could not be accomplished by Practitioner syllabus updates, so ISEB decided to create a new Intermediate level qualification to bridge the gap between Foundation and Practitioner.

ISEB introduced the Intermediate Certificate in Software Testing in 2007 to coincide with the release of the new Practitioner syllabuses, with the aim of providing the desired 'bridging' qualification between Foundation and Practitioner. The Intermediate qualification was designed to give candidates an opportunity to tackle a more advanced examination without having to assimilate a significant amount of new material. The Intermediate Certificate is a prerequisite for those seeking a Practitioner qualification.

In this introductory chapter we explain the content and structure of the Intermediate Certificate syllabus and its associated examination and provide an insight into the way the book is structured to support learning in the various syllabus areas. Finally we offer guidance on the best way to use this book, either as a learning resource or as a revision aid.

THE SOFTWARE TESTING INTERMEDIATE CERTIFICATE

Like the first level Foundation Certificate, the Intermediate Certificate provides broad coverage of the whole discipline of software testing. Unlike the Foundation, the Intermediate Certificate is aimed at those who seek a more practical treatment of the core material.

The Intermediate syllabus contains a number of learning objectives related to the analysis of testing situations, with the intention that examinations will test a candidate's ability to apply the key ideas in a practical and realistic setting. For this reason, the Intermediate examination is mainly set at the K4 level. A full explanation of K levels is contained in Appendix B, but Foundation Certificate holders will be familiar with levels K1 to K3, all of which were used in the Foundation examination. The K4 level requires candidates to be able to analyse information so that the response made to a situation is specific to that situation. In examination terms, this means that candidates will be asked to analyse scenarios and answer questions directly related to a scenario.

The authors of the syllabus have aimed it at Foundation Certificate holders, which makes the certificate accessible to those who are or who aim to be specialist testers, but also to those who require to take their more general understanding of testing to a higher level; it should therefore be appropriate to project managers, quality managers and software development managers. Although one specific aim of the Intermediate Certificate is to prepare certificate holders for the Practitioner level of certification, the Intermediate Certificate has sufficient breadth and depth of coverage to stand-alone as the next step up from the Foundation certificate.

THE INTERMEDIATE CERTIFICATE SYLLABUS

Syllabus content and structure

The syllabus is broken down into five main sections, each of which has associated with it a minimum contact time that training courses must include within any accredited training course:

- Testing fundamentals (3 hours)
- Reviews (4 hours)
- Testing and risk (3 hours)
- Test management (4 hours)
- Test analysis (4 hours)

The relative timings are a reliable guide to the amount of time that should be spent studying each section of the syllabus.

Each section of the syllabus also includes a list of learning objectives that provides candidates with a guide to what they should know when they have completed their study of a section and a guide to what can be expected to be asked in an examination. The learning objectives can be used to check that learning or revision is adequate for each topic. In the book, which is structured around the syllabus sections, we have presented the learning objectives for each section at the beginning of the relevant chapter, and the summary at the end of each chapter confirms how those learning objectives have been addressed.

Finally, each topic in the syllabus has associated with it a level of understanding, represented by the legend K1, K2, K3 or K4; these are explained in detail in Appendix B.

- Level of understanding K1 is associated with recall, so that a topic labelled K1 contains information that a candidate should be able to remember but not necessarily use or explain.
- Level of understanding K2 is associated with the ability to explain a topic or to classify information or make comparisons.
- Level of understanding K3 is associated with the ability to apply a topic in a practical setting.
- Level of understanding K4 is associated with the ability to analyse a situation and make reasoned judgements about testing in that specific situation.

The level of understanding influences the level and type of questions that can be expected to be asked about that topic in the examination.

Questions in the Intermediate examination are at the K level associated with the syllabus topic(s) covered by the question.

Syllabus map

The syllabus can usefully be viewed as a mind map, as shown in Figure I.

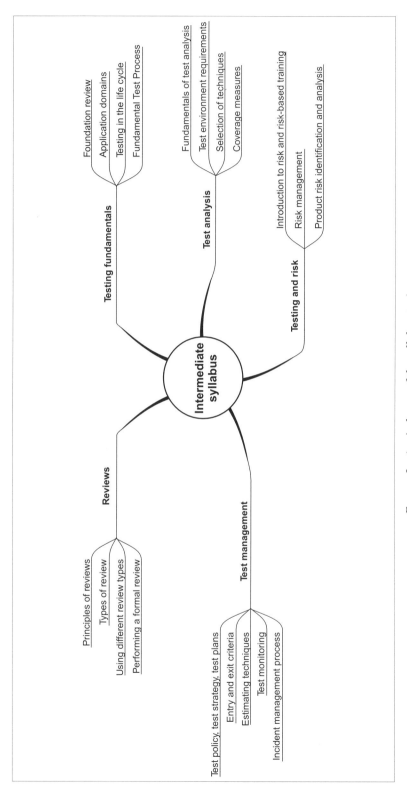

FIGURE I   *A mind map of the syllabus topics*

In this representation the main sections of the syllabus, corresponding to chapters in the book, provide the first level of ordering. The next level provides the breakdown into topics within each section. In most cases the syllabus breaks topics down even further, but the level of breakdown is omitted from the diagram for clarity. Figure I enables the entire syllabus to be viewed and is potentially useful as a tracking mechanism to identify visually which parts of the syllabus need most attention and which parts you feel are well understood. By recognising the relative strengths and weaknesses by topic within sections it is easier to understand the nature and extent of the weakness. There is relatively little new theoretical content in the Intermediate syllabus, so the main aspect to be assessed is your confidence in analysing scenarios and applying the ideas from each topic to the scenario.

THE INTERMEDIATE CERTIFICATE EXAMINATION

The Intermediate Certificate examination consists of 25 multiple choice questions. All questions are set in the context of scenarios; an examination includes five scenarios, each with five questions.

More detail about the question style and about the examination is given in Chapter 6. Example questions, written to the level and in the formats used in the examination, are included within each chapter to provide plenty of analysis practice.

RELATIONSHIP OF THE BOOK TO THE SYLLABUS

This book has been written specifically to help potential candidates for the ISEB Intermediate Certificate in Software Testing to prepare for the examination. Like its predecessor, *Software Testing: An ISEB Foundation* (2007), the book is structured to support learning of the key ideas in the syllabus quickly and efficiently for those who do not plan to attend a course, and to support structured revision for anyone preparing for the exam, whether or not they have attended a training course.

The book is structured into chapters that mirror the sections of the syllabus so that you can work your way through the whole syllabus or select topics that are of particular interest or concern. The structure enables you to go straight to the place you need, with confidence that what you need to know will either be covered there and nowhere else, or that relevant cross references will be provided.

Each chapter of the book incorporates the learning objectives from the syllabus and identifies the required level of understanding for each topic. Each chapter includes self-assessment questions to enable you to assess your current knowledge of a topic before you read the chapter; at the end of each chapter there are examples of scenario-based questions to provide practice in answering typical examination questions. Answers are provided for all questions, and the rationale for the correct answer is discussed for all practice questions.

Chapter 6 explains the Intermediate Certificate examination strategy and provides guidance on how to prepare for the examination and how to manage the examination experience to maximise your own performance.

HOW TO GET THE BEST OUT OF THIS BOOK

This book is designed for use by different groups of people. If you are using the book as an alternative to attending an accredited course you will probably find the first method of using the book described below to be of greater value. If you are using the book as a revision aid you may find the second approach more appropriate. In either case you would be well advised to acquire a copy of the syllabus (available from www.bcs.org.uk) and a copy of the sample examination paper (available from ISEB) as reference documents, though neither is essential, and the book stands alone as a learning and revision aid.

Using the book as a learning aid

For those using the book as an alternative to attending a course the first step is to familiarise yourself with the syllabus structure and content by skim reading the opening sections of each chapter where the learning objectives are identified for each topic. You may then find it helpful to turn to Chapter 6 and become familiar with the structure of the examination and the types and levels of questions that you can expect in the examination. From here you can then work through each of the five main chapters in any sequence before returning to Chapter 6 to remind yourself of the main elements of the examination.

For each chapter begin by attempting the self-assessment questions at the beginning to get initial confirmation of your level of confidence in the topics covered by that chapter. This may help you to prioritise how you spend your time. Work first through the chapters where your knowledge is weakest, attempting all the exercises and following through all the worked examples. Read carefully through the chapters where your knowledge is less weak but still not good enough to pass the exam. You can be more selective with exercises and examples here, but make sure you attempt the practice questions at the end of the chapters. For the areas where you feel strong you can use the chapter for revision but remember to attempt the practice questions to positively confirm your initial assessment of your level of knowledge. Every chapter contains a summary section that reiterates the learning objectives, so reading the first and last sections of a chapter will help you to understand how your current level of knowledge relates to the level required to pass the examination. The best confirmation of this is to attempt questions at the relevant K level for each topic; these are provided in the book. The ability to analyse situations and answer questions at the K4 level is the single most important part of preparation for the Intermediate examination. There is no level of knowledge that will substitute for this practical ability to analyse scenarios and apply the ideas explained in the book.

Using the book as a revision aid

If you are using this book for final revision, perhaps after completing an accredited course, you might like to begin by using a selection of the example questions at the end of each chapter as an initial assessment of where you are in relation to what is needed to pass the exam; this will provide you with a fairly reliable guide to your current state of readiness to take the examination. You can also discover which areas most need revision from your performance in this initial analysis, and this will guide you as you plan your revision.

Revise first where you feel weakest. You can use the opening sections of each chapter, containing the learning objectives and the self-assessment questions, together with the summary at the end of each chapter to further refine your awareness of your own weaknesses. From here you can target your studies very accurately.

You can get final confirmation of your readiness to take the real examination by taking the sample examination paper provided by ISEB.

Whatever route you take it should lead you to a confident performance in the examination and we wish you good luck with it.

Answers

Answers to chapter Checks of Understanding, Example Examination Questions, Exercises and Self-assessment Questions can be found at the end of the relevant chapter.

1 Testing fundamentals

BACKGROUND

The ISEB Foundation Certificate syllabus covered six main areas:

- Fundamentals of testing
- Testing throughout the software life cycle
- Static techniques
- Test design techniques
- Test management
- Tool support for testing

The Intermediate Certificate follows a similar structure, covering five main areas:

- Testing fundamentals
- Reviews
- Testing and risk
- Test management
- Test analysis

The topic headings reflect a slightly different organisation of ideas in the Intermediate Certificate but with broadly similar scope to the Foundation Certificate. At Intermediate level the topics are addressed at a higher cognitive level than at Foundation, for example by considering how test design techniques are selected rather than focusing on using the techniques themselves.

The Intermediate Certificate extends the testing fundamentals in the Foundation syllabus by considering the testing challenges associated with particular types of application, particular software development life cycles and particular development methods. To support this aspect of the syllabus a new topic is introduced. The section on application domains introduces four broad groups of application types and characterises them in terms of their attributes and the testing challenges they pose.

INTRODUCTION TO TESTING FUNDAMENTALS

Learning objectives

The learning objectives for this chapter are listed below. You can confirm that you have achieved these by using the self-assessment questions on page 9, the 'Check of understanding' boxes distributed through the text, and the example examination questions at the end of the chapter. The chapter summary will remind you of the key ideas.

We have given a K number to each topic to represent the level of under-standing required for that topic; for an explanation of the K numbers see Chapter 6 and Appendix B.

Review of the Foundation Certificate content
- Review the main principles and themes from relevant areas of the Foundation syllabus, all of which are considered part of the required knowledge for this syllabus. (K1)

Application domains
- Describe the similarities and differences between typical application domains. (K2)
- Identify and explain the testing challenges associated with these applic-ation domains. (K2)
- Analyse a situation to determine the testing challenges present in that scenario. (K4)

Testing in the life cycle
- Recognise and explain the relationship between testing and develop-ment. (K2)
- Identify other processes with which testing interfaces during devel-opment. (K1)
- Explain the relationships between debugging, initial testing during development, confirmation testing and regression testing. (K2)
- Explain how testing fits into sequential and iterative life cycle models. (K2)
- Describe the testing challenges associated with each life cycle and explain how these challenges can be met. (K2)
- Analyse a situation to identify the SDLC model(s) in place and select appropriate testing activities to fit with the situation and the life cycle(s) in place. (K4)

Fundamental Test Process
- Recall the Fundamental Test Process and explain how it may be deployed in different situations and within different life cycle models. (K2)

Self-assessment questions

The following questions have been designed to enable you to check your cur-rent level of understanding of the topics in this chapter. Note that they are not representative of the questions you will see in an Intermediate examination; examples of these are given at the end of the chapter. These self-assessment questions are designed to enable you to assess your knowledge of the topics covered in this chapter before you attempt any scenario-based questions.

The answers to the self-assessment questions are provided on page 37.

Question SA1

Which of the following is the best description of a client–server application?

- A. The application makes use of a web front end.
- B. There is at least one computer that provides information to other computers.
- C. There is one computer that provides information to dumb terminals.
- D. The application(s) run on a single computer.

Question SA2

Which of the following best describes a difference between a sequential development model and an iterative one?

- A. A sequential development model will always take longer than an iterative model, for a similar sized project.
- B. A sequential development model guarantees that the customer will like the product, while the iterative model does not.
- C. A sequential development model involves the users in testing mostly at the end of development, while the iterative model concentrates on the user perspective throughout development.
- D. A sequential development model requires significant regression testing, while an iterative model does not.

Question SA3

Which of the following best describes the purpose of the Fundamental Test Process?

- A. To identify the amount of testing that should take place at each test level in both sequential and iterative development models.
- B. To identify the activities required to conduct testing regardless of the test level or development life cycle.
- C. To identify the risks for a project and the activities required to manage these risks.
- D. To identify the skills required in order to conduct testing effectively.

RELEVANT FOUNDATION TOPICS

This chapter revisits the following topics from the Foundation syllabus:
- Development life cycles
- Fundamental Test Process
- Test levels
- Test types
- Maintenance testing

We will look at the topics above from a K4 perspective, analysing situations in order to understand the relevant development life cycles and test processes in place, with a view to identifying expectations and challenges associated with their use. We will cover these on pages 21–35.

APPLICATION DOMAINS

The topic of application domains has been included in the Intermediate syllabus to increase awareness of the testing challenges, not just of the functional and non-functional aspects of an application, but also of the underlying technical architecture on which the application may reside.

What is an application domain?

The term 'application domain' has been used in the Intermediate syllabus to identify a collection of applications with similar characteristics. Four application domains have been specified: PC-based; mainframe; client–server; web-based. Each of these domains implies a set of characteristics that will affect testing, and the characteristics of each domain contrast with those of the other domains.

In this chapter we describe the application domains and discuss their most significant characteristics from a testing point of view. From here we can identify the kinds of risk associated with each domain. Each domain is described in terms of its technical characteristics and the testing challenges that it generates. This is followed by the analysis of scenarios in order to recognise which application domain or domains are present and to identify the associated testing challenges.

In case you are concerned at this point, please do not worry. It will not be necessary for you to have a detailed understanding of the technical aspects of testing any specific application or application domain for the Intermediate Certificate, but it is essential to understand the key differences between domains and how these might affect testing.

We will now give you a high-level description of the technical characteristics of these domains, as required by the syllabus.

The PC-based domain

Technical characteristics of the PC-based domain

PC-based applications are those that are designed to run on a single PC or Macintosh (or any other stand-alone desktop, laptop or notebook architecture, down to and including all those mobile devices that use a Windows or similar operating system). Examples are Microsoft® Office, games software, accounting packages and the like. The key characteristic of the PC-based domain is that applications run on a relatively small general purpose computer with a relatively simple operating system.

You should be aware that this does not entirely differentiate the PC-based architectures from those used in other domains, because PC-based hardware has a very wide scope of applications from large servers to stand-alone machines. Stand-alone office machines, for example, will typically have medium-speed processors but limited networking capability, while other PC architectures may be used as network servers. Software written for stand-alone PCs may have a sophisticated user interface, while specialised software will be needed to enable PCs to act as web servers. At the server end of the PC spectrum applications will overlap with client–server systems and web-based systems. Even mainframe systems may have similar characteristics to a large array of PCs custom designed to solve a specific problem. This need not concern us because we will focus entirely on the nature of the PC-based domain as we have defined it.

As far as the syllabus and this book are concerned the testing of PC-based domains addresses the unique aspects of the single stand-alone PC typical of home users or simple office systems.

Testing challenges of the PC-based domain

The testing challenges associated with the PC-based domain include the fact that applications may need to be tested for:

- compatibility with both PC and Macintosh architectures and with a variety of operating systems;
- the ability to work alongside other applications;
- resource requirements, to ensure that they are not 'resource hungry', taking up more system resources than expected or desired.

The limited PC architecture offers relatively little support to testers wanting to run sophisticated tools or create complex test environments, especially if the application under test is using most of the system resources.

As we said earlier, PC-based hardware has a very wide scope of applications from stand-alone machines to front-end clients and back-end servers. We will discuss these application domains next.

EXERCISE 1 – PC-BASED APPLICATION

A software house is creating a new game, called *MyEcho*. It is designed for children under 16, to teach them about their carbon footprint. It starts off by taking the player through a typical day at school, at the weekend and on holiday. The player interacts by nominating the activities and modes of transport etc. At each step a carbon cost is given. The game is intended to be multi-player, but can be played stand-alone as well.

Which of the following is a challenge of testing that the game works correctly in stand-alone mode?

A. Testing that the game can be played on PCs with specified system requirements.
B. Testing that the carbon footprint calculations are correct.
C. Testing that the game is easy to play.
D. Testing that the game can be linked with other gamers.

The mainframe domain

Technical characteristics of the mainframe domain

The mainframe domain was the earliest to emerge and it has evolved over the decades, but many of its key characteristics remain the same. Early examples were typified by:

- being physically large;
- using 'dumb' terminals that input and access data, but do not process data;
- having significant processing capability, in terms of volume and speed of processing of data;
- being used as general purpose computing 'engines' running a variety of applications.

These characteristics are still often present but modern mainframes tend to be more specialised and have the following characteristics:

- High availability
- High security
- High scalability
- Limited user interface
- Very robust hardware and fault tolerance at hardware and software levels

Mainframe applications are commonly business critical, hence the need for high availability and security. Mainframe systems typically timeshare a central (host) computer, containing most of the intelligence of the system. Mainframe architectures may also utilise multiple virtual machines (i.e. multiple operating systems on a single hardware platform). Mainframe systems were originally designed to run applications in batch form (one at a time) using dumb terminals; interactive terminals and transaction-based applications are now more common. Hardware and software scalability is essential in most cases to enable growth, but there is also a need for backwards compatibility to enable critical legacy applications to be supported.

The mainframe category has become blurred because mainframe machines may be migrated for use as a server in a client–server system and some mainframe machines have been replaced by supercomputers (typically an array of powerful machines). Mainframe architectures are also now often used as web servers or as application servers with a web server to facilitate access via the internet.

Testing challenges of the mainframe domain

Mainframe systems may not always support a graphical user interface, so testing may need to be via a command line or other textual interface. This makes tests more labour intensive to set up and run. The large and complex operating systems used can make the test set up complex, and test

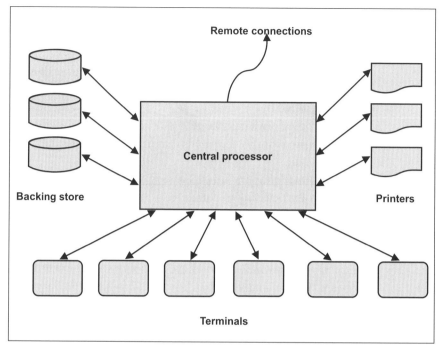

FIGURE 1.1 *Typical mainframe configuration*

environments may also be complex and may require very large databases or co-ordination between users in dispersed locations.

There are many testing challenges, including:

- creating the required test environments, which may be large and complex;
- creating and maintaining large regression test suites to support significant maintenance changes over a long time frame may be expensive and time-consuming;
- creating the large-scale test data that may be required;
- virtual machines must be tested for non-interference at the data and processing levels;
- testing for robustness and fault tolerance may require specialist skills;
- scalability testing may require costly extra hardware;
- security testing may require specialist skills and test data.

EXERCISE 2 – MAINFRAME APPLICATION

A bank is migrating its data from its current mainframe computers, to a more modern system, allowing improved data and business continuity, as part of its implementation of a disaster recovery programme. The data migration is starting with the retail arm of the bank, and will move to its investment arm, followed by other divisions. The retail banking side deals with individual and business depositors, and loans (including home loans).

Which of the following would be most important when testing the mainframe aspects of this phase of the data migration?

A. Testing that the home loan repayments are correctly calculated.

B. Testing that the integrity of the data on home loans remains intact.

C. Testing that individual customers can continue accessing their accounts online.

D. Testing that investments can continue to be made.

The client–server domain

Client–server domains are made up from a collection of 'client' computers that request services from a 'server' computer. In this context a 'client' is any computer that uses services from a 'server' and a 'server' computer is a provider of services.

The client–server architecture can be compared with the mainframe architecture, with its single time shared computer. A simple client–server architecture is depicted in Figure 1.2.

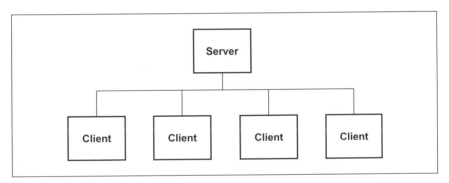

FIGURE 1.2   *The client–server application domain*

Technical characteristics of the client–server domain

- Clients and servers are remote from each other and connected by a network.
- Clients may be simple 'dumb' terminals, with no functionality of their own and acting solely as communication between client and server.
- Clients may carry out local data processing – they can be characterised as 'fat' or 'thin', depending on the amount of data processing being carried out – a PC is a typical 'fat' client.
- Clients are active components that initiate requests and wait for a response; they may be all the same or there may be differences between clients for particular users. Different clients may also have access to different services.
- Servers are passive and wait for and respond to requests.

- Servers are associated with the resource used to provide the service; this could be a large database, the internet, a group of applications, a collection of files, or any other service.

- A server is designed to manipulate the source effectively and efficiently and to respond to requests, but may not have display or other user interface functionality.

- A server would normally provide services for more than one client, with clients sending requests to the server for specific services.

- Communication between clients and servers is managed by using a network protocol that provides a standard template for all communications.

- Client–server systems are tier structured, with the server as one tier and the clients as a separate tier or tiers. It is feasible to have more than two tiers and three-tier architectures are actually quite common. For example, a three-tier architecture could have client terminals as the first tier, application servers to process data for clients as the second tier, and database servers to manage data for the applications as the third tier. This can be continued more or less indefinitely to n-tier architectures. One major advantage of increasing the number of tiers in a client–server architecture is that the tiers separate out layers of processing to better balance the load on individual servers, but the price of this is that there is more network traffic and therefore greater load on the network.

- Client–server systems are 'always on' with both clients and servers running continuously and the servers awaiting some kind of 'event' generated by a client. This is often described as an 'event-driven' architecture.

Client–server architectures have some important characteristics that make them very attractive for some kinds of applications, standing between the power and relative inflexibility of the mainframe architecture and the flexible but relatively vulnerable PC architecture.

Key advantages of client–server architectures over PC or mainframe architectures include:

- improved usability – by separating out the user interface into the client computers the usability can be enhanced at a local level;

- greater flexibility – servers or clients can be updated without affecting overall system operation;

- scalability – the architecture allows additional servers or clients to be added relatively easily;

- greater interoperability – the connections between systems can be managed at the server level.

On the negative side, traffic congestion on the network is always a potential problem. The advantage of separating out data and applications to servers also has the disadvantage that the servers become critical and any breakdown will affect the entire system.

Testing challenges of the client–server domain

- Testing a client–server system requires the creation of 'events' to exercise the event-driven architecture. This involves setting up or simulating client events, such as a request for data from a database, and then checking that the system responds correctly to each event.
- The requirement that client–server systems run continuously gives rise to new problems such as memory leaks and other dynamic effects that may cause degradation of performance over time.
- Since client–server systems contain multiple computers and networks, testing may become complicated in terms of the number of combinations of system components and interfaces to be tested.
- As for mainframes, security and performance must be given due consideration.

As a result of all these factors tests can become more complicated to set up, execute and check than for simpler architectures. Regression testing can be more difficult to automate because it can be harder to manipulate system behaviour at a local level (e.g. creating a 'server busy' condition). New kinds of defects can arise (e.g. communication problems) and performance and scalability become key characteristics that need testing.

One example of more complex testing arises because tests originating at a client (requesting a service) may fail for a large number of reasons. The test will need to ensure that all the possible responses to the request are tested, which will almost certainly mean simulating some or all of them at the client end.

EXERCISE 3 – CLIENT–SERVER APPLICATION

A client–server system has a single server providing access to a database of customer records. There are six clients in different departments, each requiring the data to be presented in a different form, so each client manipulates the data for presentation. The system requires access codes at the client sites to prevent unauthorised access to customer records.

Which of the following options best describes a testing challenge for the client–server aspects of the system?

A. Data requests will need to be generated from each client terminal to test the server's response.

B. Six testers will be required to operate each terminal simultaneously.

C. The integrity of the data stored on the database will need to be tested.

D. System testing will require a fully defined specification to be provided upfront.

The web-based domain

A web-based application is one that provides its services via a website. In some respects a web-based application is a client–server system, with a local terminal and its web browser considered as the (thin) client and the web server as the server. In this case the network is the internet and there can be a very large population of clients.

Figure 1.3 illustrates the web-based domain.

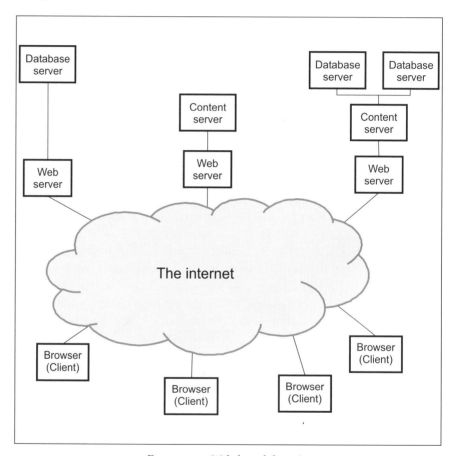

FIGURE 1.3   *Web-based domain*

Web-server architecture is mainly concerned with protocol and information retrieval interfaces on the host system. The web-server architecture uses a high-level communication layer called HyperText Transfer Protocol (HTTP); HTTP uses a reliable network transport layer called Transmission Control Protocol/Internet Protocol (TCP/IP) as the method of communication over a network.

Web-based applications are identified as a separate domain because the use of the internet as a network poses new challenges, of which the scale of the underlying network and the increased challenges of security are two fairly obvious examples.

Technical characteristics of the web-based domain

- Web applications generate documents in standard formats, such as HTML/XHTML, which are supported by all common browsers, making it very easy to update applications on the server without impact on clients.
- Web pages are generally delivered as static documents but web-form elements embedded in the page mark-up (the HTML that defines how the page is presented) can be used to make the user experience interactive.
- Web servers can be dynamically updated (e.g. when database content changes) so that user access to servers extracts the latest updated information. This is common for applications that incorporate news updates (e.g. www.bbc.co.uk).
- Problems can occur if users customise display settings or use inconsistent implementations of HTML.
- Increasingly, rich functionality at the client end is moving these applications to a 'thick' client–server. Most are three-tiered, with the browser as the user tier, dynamic web content technology (such as ASP) as a middle tier, and a database as the third tier.

There are some important consequences of these technical characteristics. For example:

- Web-based applications are essentially client–server applications running on a very large network, so they share the characteristics of client–server configurations.
- Browser-based applications use a desktop as the client with a web server as server (possibly also with a complete client–server architecture behind it).
- Dynamically generated content of web pages and dynamic database connections mean that each access to a web page may generate different results.
- Java/ActiveX content may require applets to be executed in the client environment.
- Remote application servers may sit between web servers and database servers and these may be complex.
- Some applications will bypass the web server to download directly (e.g. by using DCOM).

Testing challenges of the web-based domain

Web-based applications have all the challenges of client–server systems. In addition, they pose new problems:

- The server(s) are even more remote from the clients, which may cause issues when trying to initiate events at different tiers.
- The clients are remote from each other and may be geographically widespread.

- Client hardware architectures may have a wide variation in capability.
- Client architectures may be using a variety of operating systems and browser versions, which may increase the scope of testing.
- Increased performance testing will be required.
- Increased security testing will be required.
- Increased accessibility testing may be applicable (www.w3.org) – accessibility refers to the ability of people with disabilities to use a service.
- Increased usability testing will be required.

EXERCISE 4 – WEB-BASED APPLICATION

A global investment bank is upgrading its systems to allow its traders to access information on sales and profit performance. They will be able to access their personal performance figures, as well as those for the whole team. The system already allows traders from each country to access their own figures via an intranet. Now the information will be made available via a web interface, and is intended to allow traders to measure their performance on a global scale.

Which of the following best describes a testing challenge of the web aspects of the upgrade?

A. Testing that the traders enter their figures accurately.
B. Testing that the systems calculate individual and team performance accurately.
C. Testing that the figures are available on demand.
D. Testing that bonuses match performance.

CHECK OF UNDERSTANDING CU1

Match the testing challenge on the left to its most appropriate application domain on the right.

Testing challenge	Application domain
Generating network traffic	PC-based
Testing for different browsers	Mainframe
Operating system compatibility	Client–server
Robustness testing	Web-based

Analysing application domains

Of course real application domains are seldom, if ever, limited to one of the models we have just described. Two or more of the domain models may be in use in a real situation, and the analysis of the scenario will need to identify the dominant features so that testing decisions are targeted at those features.

A TYPICAL SCENARIO

Let us return to our game *MyEcho* that you first met in Exercise 1 on page 12.

There we saw that the game is multi-player. It can be played with other users, usually these days via a web interface. This means that we must test not just that the game can be successfully played on individual machines, but also that it can be linked with other gamers. This may require, for instance, the creation of avatars to represent the gamer online. Thus, there are two application domains present: stand-alone and web-based. Testing the avatar functionality must also include checking the ability to not just create the avatar on the user machine (a stand-alone aspect), but also to upload it for use online (a web-based aspect).

Later we will extend the analysis to include software development life-cycle models and development approaches, which are the other main factors to be considered in selecting a testing approach in a given scenario.

SOFTWARE DEVELOPMENT MODELS, TEST LEVELS AND TEST TYPES

Software development life cycles

The Foundation syllabus included an outline of the two generic life cycles: sequential, using the V life cycle as an example, and iterative. The V life cycle, shown in Figure 1.4 in one of its many possible manifestations, is often used as an ideal model because of the very structured way that development and testing are related.

This is an idealised model in many respects and is seldom replicated in practice. It provides a clear and simple way to describe the relationship between testing and development, by showing that each development activity has an associated testing activity, and by demonstrating that tests can and should be specified at the same time as the associated development deliverable is created. Why? Because the activity of specifying tests is an excellent way of testing the quality of the development deliverable. Any problems with creating tests signal similar problems with the next step in development and these problems are better sorted out early. A full implementation of this model would have reviews at every stage and test specifications created before module coding begins.

In practice this model has some fundamental problems, most important of which is the fact that the whole model depends on the quality and completeness of the requirements, since both the testing and development activities stem from this single deliverable. Requirements are notoriously difficult to

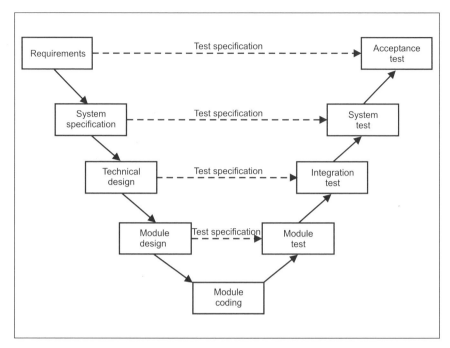

FIGURE 1.4   *The V life cycle*

define and usually do not remain stable throughout a software project, so this model is usually compromised in practice.

The iterative model (Figure 1.5) takes the idea that requirements are seldom stable to its logical conclusion and removes the dependence on stable requirements by not attempting to define them fully at the beginning of the project. Instead it identifies a set of objectives for the project and prioritises these. The development is then split into a series of short timeboxes, during which a subset of the requirements is developed and tested, so that the project progresses as a series of short development cycles, each focused on the highest priority requirements not yet developed.

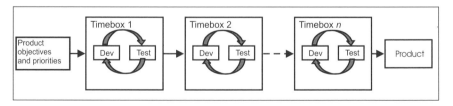

FIGURE 1.5   *The iterative life cycle*

The aim of iterative development is to ensure that the highest priority requirements are developed first and to reduce the burden of verification, which is the emphasis in the V model. Iterative development, then, aims for maximum visibility of product quality; this usually involves continuous customer involvement throughout the entire development cycle.

This model also has its drawbacks. The very light verification process has the consequences that specifications and systematic testing do not often feature very highly. Validation of functionality, often by customers, is carried out at each iteration. Typically, the lack of detailed requirements limits the use of systematic test design techniques (in particular those requiring detailed specifications, such as equivalence partitioning). In addition, the focus on subsets of requirements can impair the overall design.

Examples of iterative development models are: Rapid Application Development (RAD), Prototyping, Agile, Dynamic Systems Development Methodology (DSDM).

This brief overview of testing in alternative life cycles shows that each model has its benefits and drawbacks. Practical testing, like practical development, involves compromise and choice.

The focus of the Intermediate Certificate is to consider how testing processes can be integrated most effectively with development processes to minimise the inherent problems and maximise the opportunities to identify and remove defects.

Test levels and test types

Test level is simply a way of referring to any group of test activities that are organised and managed together.

In the V life cycle, test level relates to the testing associated with each development work product, such as component testing or integration testing. In this case the idea of level is naturally associated with the point in the life cycle where testing occurs.

In an iterative life cycle test levels would occur at the end of each timebox, where all the functionality developed in that timebox is tested together and with functionality developed in earlier timeboxes.

Test type refers to test activities directed towards achieving a particular test objective, so functional testing and performance testing are both examples of test types. Any test type can occur at any test level and may occur at more than one test level. Functional testing is likely to occur at every test level, whereas performance testing is more likely to occur at some test levels than at others e.g. more at system test level than at component test level.

Testing activities in the life cycle

The relationship between testing, development and other disciplines within the overall development life cycle is a complex one. In this section we will consider the relationship between testing and some of the many alternative ways of developing software to provide a framework for assessing how this relationship can be optimised. We will also consider how software testing relates to the other key disciplines that interface with development.

First of all, we return to the familiar V life cycle, where the relationship between testing and development is simple and consistent. For every development work product there are two corresponding test activities: one to determine the quality of the work product itself, including its testability, and one to specify the testing to be carried out on the software defined by the work product. When the software is constructed a third test activity executes the tests. This is shown for a single work product in Figure 1.6.

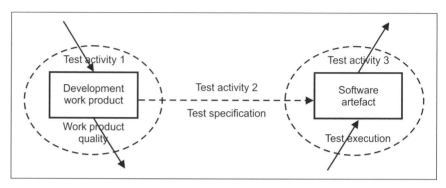

FIGURE 1.6   *Testing activities in the V life cycle*

Each level in the V life cycle will have a similar relationship between work product, software artefact and test activities, but the details of the test specifications will be different for each level.

In an iterative life cycle with time boxed development the picture is rather different. Each timebox represents a complete 'life cycle' from requirements through to software product but for a limited set of requirements. The relationship between development and testing is shown in Figure 1.7.

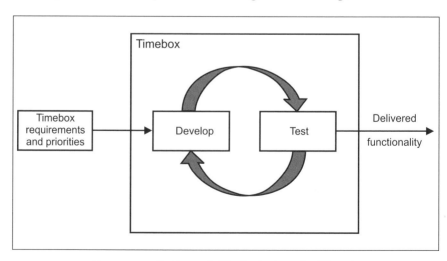

FIGURE 1.7   *Testing activities in the iterative life cycle*

Figure 1.7 represents a single timebox; a complete project would consist of a sequence of timeboxes, each with a new set of requirements. Note that testing is continuous and related to validating timebox requirements.

LIFE CYCLE CHALLENGES

V model

- Defining requirements fully upfront.
- Managing change requests throughout the life cycle.
- Getting developers and testers interested and involved in reviews early.
- Balancing cost of writing tests against a test basis that may be changed downstream.
- Gaining acceptance of the system by the end users.

Iterative model

- Planning without fully defined requirements.
- Designing tests without complete specifications.
- Establishing a baseline for regression testing.
- Sourcing staff with strong technical and business domain skills.
- Keeping items under configuration management.

Life cycle related testing challenges

The testing challenges generated by alternative life cycles can now be identified as a set of inherent risks that will need to be accounted for in any test plan.

In a sequential life cycle a significant challenge is the management of change. The dependence on complete and correct requirements is a problem that, in practice, leads to change throughout the life cycle as new requirements emerge. This means that test plans must try to estimate and allow for this unknown activity and its impact on testing. Another difficult area is the unknown quality of the work products because lower quality will generate a greater burden of confirmation and regression testing as well as causing delays while defects are corrected. The issue of quality is a serious one. A project team's familiarity with a set of requirements or the best way to create an application to meet those requirements will be key factors in determining the quality of work products; an inexperienced team or one working in a new application environment can be expected to generate lower quality in the sense that work products will contain more defects.

In an iterative life cycle the challenges are mostly associated with the timeboxed approach, both because of the limitations that are placed on the time available for testing and because the product is often built with minimal documentation (usually outline requirements). The idea of building test specifications in advance from detailed work product specifications is often not tenable. One response to this problem has been an approach known as test-driven development. This is a method of software design in which the test procedures for the iteration are written before the code is created. This has the advantage at this stage of enabling better software design by understanding what it should do from a user perspective. The code is then created and tested against the test procedures already written, and released once the tests have been passed. This is one innovative way in which the inability to construct detailed test scripts from specifications has been tackled.

Whatever the nature of the life cycle, there will be some testing challenges that generate inherent risk for the test strategy to address. In practice the 'pure' V life cycle is as uncommon as the 'pure' iterative life cycle. Both are idealised models, which can be tailored to meet the challenges of particular projects.

CHECK OF UNDERSTANDING CU2

1. Which development model relies on requirements being captured as fully as possible at the very start of the project?
2. Which development model relies on user validation throughout?
3. Give two benefits of the V model.
4. Give two benefits of the iterative model.
5. Give two testing challenges of the V model.
6. Give two testing challenges of the iterative model.

Testing and development

So far we have considered 'vanilla-flavoured' development, or development in the absence of any particular development environment. The V life cycle, for example, assumes that requirements are functionally decomposed and modules of software constructed to meet each decomposed function in some kind of top down approach. Is software actually constructed that way? Not very often.

In practice, software is constructed using technology to support and, wherever possible, automate the development processes in a development environment. Development methodologies are many and varied but they each bring their own advantages and disadvantages from a testing perspective. We will here consider three alternatives that broadly represent the main ways in which development is made more productive and less risky; these examples can then serve as a template for assessing the impact of development methodologies and technology on the testing activities.

Our examples will be:

- object-oriented development;
- development using reused software components;
- construction of systems from commercial off-the-shelf (COTS) software.

Object-oriented software development

Object-oriented software development was created as a means to maintaining software quality, as systems increased in complexity. A key feature in object-oriented development is the organisation of the code into discrete classes that contain both data structures and the procedures that operate on them, as an alternative to defining procedures and data structures separately. The classes then have limitations on how they can be used and manipulated, leading to the core concept of information hiding.

Information hiding means that data in a system can only be accessed via specific access methods provided by the system. In other words the tester cannot arbitrarily amend data fields to set up tests.

Testing of object-oriented systems therefore entails harnessing the object-oriented development system to testing by constructing 'test objects' that utilise the access methods of objects in the system and encapsulate the test scripts within the test object's own methods.

This is one relatively simple example of the impact of development methodologies, especially those supported by technology, which may demand from the tester a more detailed understanding of the underlying development methodology and technology.

Software reuse

Software reuse involves the storing and reuse of software components that perform tasks likely to be required in other projects. When a requirement for the task arises the existing component is reused in preference to constructing a new component. There are a number of advantages to this, perhaps the most important being reduced effort and the reduced risk in using a 'tried and tested' component. From a testing perspective, however, this approach creates new challenges.

- A reused component will have been tested in its original environment, which is unlikely to be identical to the environment into which it will now be introduced.
- It is also possible that the reused component may need to be modified to fit the exact requirements of the new task. Thus the modifications will also need to be tested and monitored to ensure that they do not equate to a new piece of code, requiring more extensive testing than at first thought.

ARIANE 5 – A CASE OF POOR TESTING?

The destruction of Ariane 5 after about 40 seconds of its maiden flight on 4 June 1996 is well documented. The cause was a failure of the flight control system, leading to swivelling of the solid booster and engine nozzles, which in turn caused the vehicle to veer off its intended flight path and trigger self-destruction.

The flight control system failure was caused by a software defect but investigation showed that no software failed to perform its intended function. A module reused from the earlier Ariane 4 vehicle generated a software exception that led to the failure of both inertial reference systems (SRIs) on board and transmission to the on-board computer of diagnostic data that, when interpreted as flight data by the on-board computer, caused the demand for nozzle movements that led to the destruction of the vehicle. The reused module functioned correctly throughout but had never been exposed to the countdown and flight-time sequence and the trajectory of Ariane 5; that of Ariane 4 was different.

The testing of Ariane 5 was conducted at four levels, with each level checking what could not be checked at the previous levels. This standard approach was conducted rigorously but did not include a test that the SRI would behave correctly when being subjected to the countdown and flight-time sequence and the trajectory of Ariane 5. The test was not performed because the specification for the SRI did not contain the Ariane 5 trajectory data as a functional requirement.

This is a greatly simplified version of the official report's findings but it demonstrates that even reused software that functions correctly can be the cause of a serious failure that rigorous testing based on the requirements may still fail to predict. In this case the best tool for discovering the predictable but not obvious limitations of the reused software would have been reviews; reviews were conducted but did not discover the limitations.

Bad testing? That would be a harsh judgement, but the failure could have been averted by testing if the right tests had been designed.

Reuse of software generates new and different testing challenges that require the tester to consider carefully what risks may arise from the proposed reuse and what potential problems need to be considered in designing tests.

Implementing COTS

The main advantage of COTS is that it provides a complete solution to a business problem, usually built by domain experts and used by many other organisations. The confidence this gives in the effectiveness and reliability of the application is potentially very valuable.

In reality, however, COTS may provide a complete or a partial solution to a particular set of requirements. In most cases the fit between a COTS solution and the user community's requirements is not exact and some modification is required. Organisations may be able to modify their business processes to fit the application as built, but this will necessitate careful testing of the application in its new process environment. Commonly, the COTS software is itself modified to meet the needs of the organisation. In this case, the functionality of the modified software will need to be tested as well as its fit within the new process environment.

The main challenge here is that, even though a COTS application may have been thoroughly tested in a number of different implementations, it is unlikely that any of these will be identical to that now envisaged. Any mismatch between the new environment and those encountered before can throw up anomalous behaviour and identifying where in the application this might occur is not an easy task. A carefully planned and designed test of the application in its new environment is therefore needed. This is an exercise that has some similarities with defining a regression test suite.

In testing COTS-based systems the following are usually required by the customer:

- Acceptance testing of the package in its new environment, if unmodified.
- Where modified by the supplier, acceptance testing of original functionality and integration testing of modifications with original functionality.
- Where modified by the buyer, acceptance testing of original functionality, full testing of modifications, and integration testing of modifications with original functionality.

Of course, it is expected that the supplier will conduct full testing of all software supplied.

CHECK OF UNDERSTANDING CU3

1. In what type of development could information hiding pose a challenge in testing?
2. Identify a potential benefit of reusing software.
3. Identify a potential drawback of reusing software.
4. Identify two challenges of COTS-based development.

Testing and other project processes

Software development projects involve a myriad of overlapping and interconnecting processes. Overall there will be a project management process, the purpose of which is to ensure that the project is completed successfully and within the constraints of the project. Project management will determine how much resource is dedicated to testing and when (even if) testing will happen. Within project management the risk management discipline will identify and quantify the risks that will be a major driver of the testing effort. The relationship between testing and project management is such that project management enables testing to take place, while testing provides information about quality and remaining risk enabling the project manager to make informed decisions on software release.

Managing change involves various processes, such as change management, configuration management and requirements management. These all need to interface with testing so that changes can be incorporated into the testing plan. Any change will require an assessment of impact that may lead to variations in the test plan to test new requirements, test corrections after defect corrections or regression test after changes have been incorporated. Changes to hardware or business processes may also invalidate testing already completed, so all processes that involve change should be linked with testing so that any change can be reviewed.

Other areas that support the project, such as technical support and technical writing, will also need an interface with testing. Manuals will need to be included in testing at some stage in the project to ensure that testing correctly reflects the user procedures described in them. Technical support may be involved in building or supporting test environments and software builds for testing.

In an iterative life cycle the processes may not be so distinct. The team members may take on different roles at different times, blurring the distinctions between roles such as project manager, configuration manager and tester.

> **CHECK OF UNDERSTANDING CU4**
>
> List three other project processes that interact with the testing process.

TESTING, MAINTENANCE AND CHANGE

Testing and change

Testing, if it is effective, will find defects and thus generate change to the software and the requirements.

In a sequential life cycle, in which tight control is maintained over work products at every stage, we will need to recognise four distinct activities:

- Debugging, though not strictly testing at all, will be the first level of defect removal. Debugging will normally be done by the development team and typically will not be documented; neither will the debugged code be under project version control at this stage (though the development team should be providing local version control). Debugging is preparation for testing, seeking to bring software to a state where formal testing can begin.

- Initial testing is the execution of the tests specified in the appropriate test specification and is part of every test level. The initial tests will typically uncover a number of defects.

- Confirmation testing is the testing carried out after defects have been corrected to ensure that the corrected module now passes the initial test(s) that it failed at the first pass.

- Regression testing is the testing carried out to check that changes such as defect corrections have not made any unexpected and unwanted changes to any other area of the system.

Any change to a system will generate new or modified initial tests and associated confirmation and regression tests, which is one good reason for minimising change to requirements.

In an iterative life cycle the control of individual changes may be less formal within a timebox, allowing multiple revisions to code and test throughout the timebox. At the end of the timebox, however, the configuration of the software and the tests carried out on the software will need to be brought under control. Once a timebox has completed a controlled version of the product will be created. Future timeboxes, then, will generate regression tests to ensure that earlier tested versions of the product have not been compromised, and may require confirmation testing if earlier tested versions of the product are subsequently modified in later timeboxes.

> **CHECK OF UNDERSTANDING CU5**
>
> What is the difference between debugging and confirmation testing?

Testing and software maintenance

Maintenance is defined as everything that happens to a software product after its initial development, so most of a software product's life is in maintenance of one kind or another. Maintenance can vary from simple defect correction arising from user routine reporting, through to emergency defect correction when something goes seriously wrong in a critical area, to major enhancements of core functionality. If a maintenance activity is large and costly enough it will most probably be managed as a new project, but usually maintenance work will involve making relatively small changes to the system or product.

The problem with small changes is that they do not necessarily imply small impact on the software, so the first task is to try to discover exactly what the likely impact is, by studying the documentation if any has survived or by examining the code. Once the impact is understood a test plan can be constructed to address the risks associated with making the required change(s). This will try to restrict testing to areas where some impact is expected or at least considered possible, but in many cases this will not be feasible and the whole system may need to be tested. Since maintenance involves change, the testing regime will need to include testing of any new functionality and regression testing of potentially impacted areas. The regression tests may need to incorporate non-functional as well as functional testing. A risk-based strategy is usually the best approach in this situation and the risks will be determined by an impact analysis.

THE FUNDAMENTAL TEST PROCESS

The most important tool the tester has for coping with the many variations and challenges of life cycles, development environments and the like is the Fundamental Test Process that was introduced in the Foundation syllabus.

Test processes

The Fundamental Test Process is a set of steps showing the core activities of testing in any context; it is a reminder that we omit any of the five stages shown in Figure 1.8 at our peril.

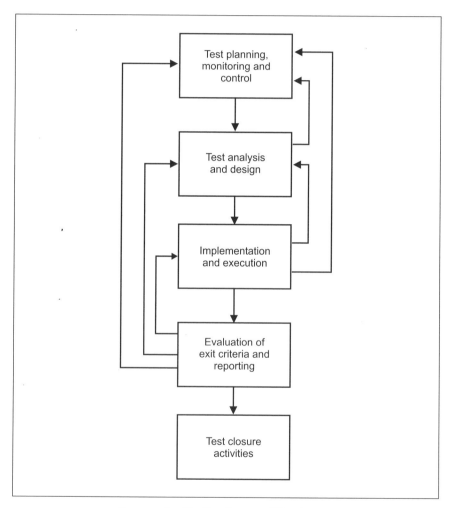

FIGURE 1.8   *The Fundamental Test Process*

The Fundamental Test Process is clearly linear, though with some important feedback loops.

The process begins with planning; this includes setting up the monitoring and control mechanisms that will be needed to ensure the process is effective. Most importantly, test planning includes the setting of test objectives and the setting of the criteria by which we will judge testing to be complete. The completion criteria reflect the level of acceptable risk while the feedback loops are included to ensure that testing is always directed at the test objectives and judged by progress towards the completion criteria. Setting the criteria at the beginning of testing ensures that we are not intimidated into inappropriate criteria when pressure may be mounting at the end of the process.

The process continues by identifying the key stages of defining test conditions and test cases, designing test scripts, executing them and determining whether the test has passed or failed, after which the status of testing against the completion criteria is assessed and decisions taken about the next step. The feedback loops enable the scope of testing to be adjusted according to the evidence provided by test results and any residual risks.

The Fundamental Test Process should be applied at every level of testing, so we would expect to see evidence of every stage in this process in a project test plan but also in each level test plan, though some activities will be more prominent than others at different levels (thus we would not expect to see a full test plan at unit testing).

In the following sections we consider how the Fundamental Test Process relates to the life cycles and development methodologies we have considered in earlier sections.

The Fundamental Test Process and the V model

Implementation of the Fundamental Test Process in the V life cycle is the most straightforward; a single process extends from test planning at the requirements stage to evaluation of exit criteria at acceptance and this embodies all the test phases, so the test planning step is the project test planning step. The Fundamental Test Process also applies to every test level, with test planning for that level initiated at the appropriate level on the left-hand side of the V and evaluation of exit criteria happening at the appropriate level on the right-hand side of the V. In this way each test level is planned, designed, executed and evaluated in its own right, and achievement of its exit criteria is a prerequisite for entering the next test level. The complete set of level entry and exit criteria will be documented in the project test plan. Failure to meet exit criteria requires a decision at the appropriate test level and also at the overall project level, so that risks are managed at the test level but any risk remaining from a test level is taken into account at the project level.

The Fundamental Test Process and the iterative model

The iterative model poses a different process challenge. In this life cycle there are no hierarchical levels but a sequence of timeboxed developments. Here the Fundamental Test Process applies to the project as a whole and will include the overall structure of timeboxes, with their generic entry and exit criteria. Phases such as test analysis and design, and implementation and execution, may be combined to reflect the testing approach adopted, but the evaluation of testing against criteria to determine when testing is complete will still be a key feature at the end of the project. In this case the Fundamental Test Process will be applied in exactly the same form to each timebox, but the final details of entry and exit conditions may be deferred until just before the timebox begins, when the objectives of the timebox are known.

The Fundamental Test Process is a very important part of preventing the testing in an iterative life cycle degenerating into a secondary or overhead activity under time pressures, and it is in this kind of situation that a well-defined process adds most value.

The Fundamental Test Process and development

The variations in approach brought about by the use of particular development methods may have a significant impact on individual test activities or the scope and content of test levels, but we would not expect the Fundamental Test Process to be overridden or significantly modified. For example, the incorporation of reused components may make the component testing level less significant but this may be balanced by a more extensive integration testing level. Both levels would still be planned and implemented using the Fundamental Test Process as a template.

In the case of COTS the variation may be greater. If COTS is being used to provide a complete application, testing may be effectively reduced to two levels: a brief system test to confirm functionality, and some kind of acceptance test that determines the correctness and effectiveness of the COTS application with business processes, especially if the latter have been modified. The acceptance activity may be extensive and may be expected to find defects, so the careful planning and management of the test process, at both levels and as a project, will be of major importance to the success of the COTS implementation. The main point here, though, is that the testing should still use the Fundamental Test Process as a template for the activity.

CHECK OF UNDERSTANDING CU6

1. Draw a representation of the V model, showing where the Fundamental Test Process fits in.
2. Repeat the above for an iterative development model.

SCENARIO ANALYSIS

The first task of the specialist tester is to analyse not only the application domain, the specific application under test and the product risks but also the life cycle, the development environment, and any other factor that will impact on the nature and extent of testing required to reduce the risk to an acceptable level. Each of these factors needs to be taken into account. You also need to consider the overall scenario by assigning weights to the various factors so that you can come to a balanced view of the scenario as a whole. From this balanced view you can identify the most significant factors for selecting and deploying the optimum testing approach.

In exam questions the scenarios will clearly signal the various factors but you will need to draw from them your own balanced view. The questions will provide choices for the way to handle the testing challenges with some explanation of the reasoning so that you can select the right response with the right reason and reject incorrect responses or those for which the reason given is not valid.

Exercise 5 should help to clarify how scenario analysis works.

EXERCISE 5 – A TYPICAL SCENARIO

An online book selling company is enhancing its offerings to include sourcing out-of-print books, for specialist interest groups (SIGs). It is already providing access to books on aviation, and is about to start on bird watching, with other topics to be added later on demand. The system includes an invitation to current SIG members to register their interest. On registration, customers are sent an instruction sheet on how to use the system. Development is carried out using Agile methods, in line with company standards.

The development team intends to adapt the software used for aviation books for use in sourcing bird watching books. In addition, the site will now include links to countrywide SIGs.

Which two of the following are challenges most likely to arise specifically out of the life cycle in use?

i. Testers may not be able to review the specification for the bird watching book offerings fully at the start of development.

ii. Testers may not fully understand how the enthusiasts are likely to use the site.

iii. Testers may not become involved in the creation of the instruction sheet on how to use the system.

iv. A defect found and fixed at iteration n may become a defect again at iteration $n + 1$ because of changing requirements.

A. i, ii
B. i, iii
C. iii, iv
D. ii, iv

SUMMARY

In this chapter we have reviewed the relevant testing fundamentals from the Foundation syllabus and extended them to provide a greater awareness of the challenges in testing particular software development life cycles and development approaches. We have also introduced the main application domains and examined the challenges in testing these. We have reviewed the Fundamental Test Process and considered how it applies to the two main life-cycle models that we have examined: the sequential V life cycle and the iterative life cycle.

The chapter has also introduced the kind of scenarios and scenario-based questions from which the Intermediate Certificate examination is constructed and provided some initial practice in analysing scenarios and tackling scenario-based questions.

A mind map of the content of the chapter is in Appendix A.

EXAMPLE EXAMINATION QUESTIONS

A website building company (WBC) specialises in building websites for clients with existing database-driven systems. Their clients include those in the real estate, recruitment and mailing list businesses.

The company has been asked to build a new website for a major recruitment agency (RA) that has offices around the world. The agency has a database of over 5,000 firms, and holds CVs on over 100,000 candidates. Access to the current site is by permission level, with firms having access to one part, candidates another, and in-house staff another.

WBC uses object-oriented methods and the Agile model for development, and prides itself in the quality of its products. It uses its standard COTS product, and customises it for each client. However, it has been taken over recently, and many of the development staff have left. It is currently undertaking its own recruitment drive to find new staff.

RA is concerned that its corporate branding is retained, and that its staff and customers instantly identify with the new website, while enjoying a fresh online experience. However, it is keen to get the new site up and running as quickly as possible, and expects to double its firm and candidate list in the next year.

WBC will build the system in two iterations: front-end development followed by integration with the back-end.

E1

Which of the following are testing challenges associated with the integration of the new website with the back-end database?

i.   Testing that the new website reflects RA's branding.

ii. Testing that the new website retains the current access levels.

   iii. Testing that the integrity of the data on firms and candidates is not compromised.

   iv. Monitoring the number of hits to the new website.

   A. i and ii

   B. i and iii

   C. ii and iii

   D. ii and iv

E2

Which of the following is a testing challenge associated with the development methodology?

   A. Performance testing to cope with the doubling of clients.

   B. Information hiding, necessitating the creation of test objects.

   C. Navigation testing of the new website.

   D. Training new staff in reviewing specifications quickly.

E3

Which of the following steps in the Fundamental Test Process is most likely to be reduced in this scenario?

   A. Planning of how long testing of the iteration for the back-end integration will take.

   B. Design of tests required for the back-end integration.

   C. Running tests on the changes to the back-end interface after integration.

   D. Evaluation of suitability of the website to RA's needs before moving on to the back-end integration.

E4

Which of the following levels of testing would RA be recommended to perform on WBC's core product prior to the customisations?

   A. Full testing on the core product.

   B. Acceptance testing on the core product.

   C. Regression testing after customisation.

   D. Unit testing on the customisations.

ANSWERS TO SELF-ASSESSMENT QUESTIONS (ON PAGE 10)

SA1. B

SA2. C

SA3. B

ANSWERS TO CHECKS OF UNDERSTANDING

CU1 (on page 20)

In the table below we have reordered the entries in the right-hand column to match the most appropriate application domain to the testing challenge.

Testing challenge	Application domain
Generating network traffic	Client–server
Testing for different browsers	Web-based
Operating system compatibility	PC-based
Robustness testing	Mainframe

Note that in testing, we would aim to test all aspects of a system relating to each application domain present. Here we have looked at what our focus would be when testing against each application domain.

CU2 (on page 26)

1. The V model requires requirements to be fully captured at the start of a project.
2. The iterative model (e.g. Agile development) relies on continual user validation of product functionality during the project.
3. Two benefits of the V model: tests are created as soon as specifications are written, thus defects in the specifications can be identified before coding begins; model shows explicitly the levels of testing to be undertaken at each stage of development.
4. Two benefits of the iterative model: provision is made for requirements to be changed by the customer, thus reducing the risk that the end product may not meet their needs; the customer has early visibility of the working product, allowing them to highlight deficiencies as the product is being built, again reducing the risk of rejection at release.
5. Two testing challenges of the V model: tests created at the start of development may need to be changed downstream; validation at the end of development may lead to customers not fully accepting the system.
6. Two testing challenges of the iterative model: the frequency of requirements changes may lead to an onerous amount of regression testing; lack of detailed specifications may lead to poor test design, thus key defects may be missed.

Here we have listed some key benefits and challenges associated with linear and iterative software development models. Hopefully you have added some more of your own.

CU3 (on page 29)

1. Object-oriented software development makes use of information hiding, which may create a testing challenge.
2. A potential benefit of reusing software is that less effort may be required for testing.

3. A potential drawback of reusing software is that the reused component may need to be modified in order to integrate it into a new environment. This could cause an increased need for testing, which may not be obvious, leading to defects being missed.

4. A challenge of COTS-based development is similar to that of reusing software, it may not work as expected in its new environment. Another is identifying whether defects identified lie within the customised software or in the original functionality.

CU4 (on page 30)

Project processes interacting with the testing process include:
- configuration management
- technical authoring
- technical support
- risk management
- project management.

(Note that we have given more processes than the question has asked for.)

CU5 (on page 31)

The difference between debugging and confirmation testing is that debugging is the process of removing a defect, while confirmation testing is the process of confirming that the fix has been applied correctly.

CU6 (on page 34)

1.

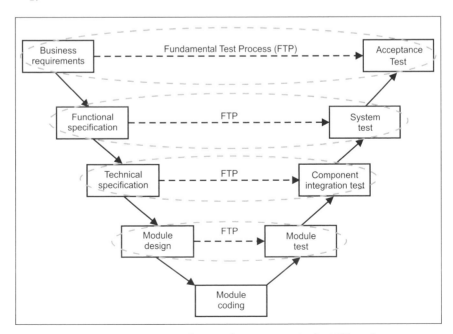

FIGURE 1.9 *The Fundamental Test Process in the V life cycle*

Here we see that we should undertake all steps of the Fundamental Test Process, from planning and test design through to test closure at every level of testing in the V model. Note that we are not suggesting that the full process must be followed at the lower levels of testing. However, there must be some element of planning, test design etc.

2.

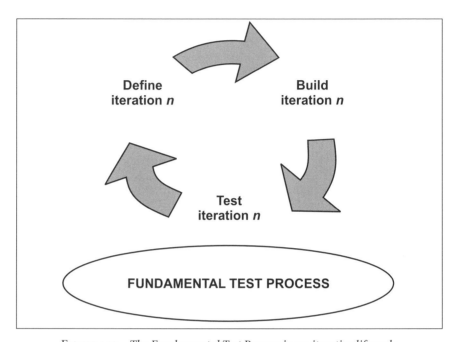

FIGURE 1.10   *The Fundamental Test Process in an iterative life cycle*

Here we see that the Fundamental Test Process should apply throughout each iteration. Note that the absence of fully defined specifications may make test design difficult, but the method used should be documented.

ANSWERS TO EXERCISES

Exercise 1 (on page 12)

The correct answer is A.

Answer B is incorrect because the calculation of the carbon footprint is associated with testing the application itself, not the underlying technical architecture on which the application resides.

Answer C is incorrect because testing whether the game is easy or not, once again depends on the requirements of the application itself, not the application domain.

Answer D is incorrect because linking the game to other players would not be associated with the game being used in stand-alone mode.

Exercise 2 (on page 14)

The correct answer is B.

Answer A is a tempting option, since it is possible that the calculation algorithms may become corrupted on the migration. However, it is not as good as B, because it is considering just one aspect of data integrity, while answer B considers all of the data.

Answer C is relevant in testing, but is not part of mainframe data testing, and thus is incorrect.

Answer D should be a clear distracter. The first phase will deal with the retail arm of the business, and the scenario gives no information on how investments are made. Thus this is incorrect.

Exercise 3 (on page 17)

The correct answer is A.

Answer B is incorrect because the number six refers to the number of client machines, not the number of testers. What will be of interest is the number of requests that can be handled from the servers simultaneously. Typically, a performance test tool will be used to generate the requests, not testers.

Answer C is incorrect because this is a challenge of testing the database itself, not the client–server part of the system.

Answer D is incorrect because this is a challenge associated with testing any system, not specifically any particular part of it (and sadly, we're aware that we often don't have these, whatever we're testing!).

Exercise 4 (on page 20)

The correct answer is C.

Answer A is incorrect because the system as described makes no mention of checking accuracy of data entered.

Answer B is incorrect because testing of the calculations would form part of the testing of the functionality of the application itself, not its use online.

Answer D is incorrect because the scenario gives no indication that bonuses are calculated in the system. In addition, this calculation, if it existed, would form part of the application testing, as for answer B.

Exercise 5 (on page 35)

The correct answer is D.

The scenario presents a number of factors:

- The application is online (so web-based).
- It will use Agile (iterative) methods.
- It involves adapting an existing application and extending it to include new functionality (links to SIGs).

The question, however, focuses on the life cycle model in use. In other words, it is asking for you to identify two challenges most likely when using an iterative model. Let us look at each possible option in turn.

i.   This suggests that specifications will be available and that testers will need to be able to review them fully. This is more applicable to the use of the V model, but for now let's leave it in as an option, since it is not impossible in an iterative model.

ii. This is looking at the end-user perspective and is applicable in iterative developments, so this can be a possible answer.

iii. This may be useful, but would be a challenge in any life-cycle model, therefore we can rule it out. This is because the question asks for challenges specific to the iterative model.

iv. This is very likely in iterative development, where requirements are expected to change significantly.

We have now ruled out option iii as a possible answer.

We need to rule out another. Option i is quite unlikely when compared with options ii and iv. Therefore, we can rule out option i, leaving us with options ii and iv.

ANSWERS TO EXAMPLE EXAMINATION QUESTIONS

E1 (on page 36)

The correct answer is C: activities ii and iii.

i.   Testing that the new website reflects RA's branding is part of the functional testing of the website, it is not associated with integration.

iv. Monitoring the number of hits to the new website is also not part of integration testing of the front and back ends.

E2 (on page 37)

The correct answer is B.

Answer A is about performance testing, which is independent of the development methodology.

Answer C is about navigation testing. As for performance testing, this is independent of the development methodology.

Answer D should be a clearly incorrect answer. This is outside the scope of test execution.

E3 (on page 37)

The correct answer is B.

Answer A, test planning, should not be reduced.

Answer B, test design, relies on detailed specifications. These are unlikely to be available in an Agile environment.

Answer C, test execution, is a given and should not be reduced.

Answer D, evaluation of the functionality against the user needs is a key consideration in testing in an Agile environment.

E4 (on page 37)

The correct answer is B.

Answer A, full testing of the core product should be carried out by WBC, not RA.

Answer C refers to regression testing after customisation. The question asks for testing required before customisation.

Answer D refers to unit testing on the customisation. This would be carried out by WBC, not RA. In addition, as for answer C, the question relates to the core product before customisations.

2 Reviews

BACKGROUND

Reviews play an increasingly important role in software testing. As complexity and size of software systems grow inexorably, so do the cost and difficulty of dynamic testing.

Static testing, including reviews, can provide a cost-effective way of preventing defects downstream, where, as is generally accepted, they would be more expensive to fix than if they were addressed earlier in the life cycle.

The Ariane 5 case study, which was outlined in Chapter 1 (page 27), provided a very clear example of a situation in which effective reviewing could have avoided a disastrous outcome, that dynamic testing failed to detect prior to launch.

Reviewing is so central to software testing that both test managers and test analysts need a sound working knowledge of principles and practice. This chapter adds some of the practical detail needed to make review activities effective and includes an approach to gaining the practical experience of reviewing that is essential to a real understanding of the strengths and weaknesses of reviews.

INTRODUCTION TO REVIEWS

Learning objectives

The learning objectives for this chapter are listed below. You can confirm that you have achieved these by using the self-assessment questions on page 45, the 'Check of understanding' boxes distributed through the text, and the example examination questions at the end of the chapter. The chapter summary will remind you of the key ideas.

We have given a K number to each topic to represent the level of understanding required for that topic; for an explanation of the K numbers see Chapter 6 and Appendix B.

Review of Foundation Certificate content
- Review the main principles and themes from relevant areas of the Foundation syllabus, all of which are considered part of the required knowledge for this syllabus. (K1)

The principles of reviews
- Recall the basic review process as defined in the Foundation syllabus. (K1)
- Explain the value of using source documents in reviews. (K2)

- Describe possible outcomes from a review. (K2)
- Recall different roles that may be defined for a particular review. (K1)
- Recall that reviews may come in a variety of forms and have different objectives. (K1)

Types of review

- Describe alternative types of formal review. (K2)
- Explain the value of informal reviews. (K2)

Using different review types

- Describe how more than one type of review could be used. (K2)
- Describe the relationship of reviews to dynamic testing. (K2)
- Analyse organisations and situations to enable the best choice of review type(s) to be made. (K4)

Performing a formal review

- Provide practical experience of conducting a formal review. (K3)
- Analyse the effectiveness of the review performed and use the analysis to assess the potential effectiveness of other forms of review in a similar situation. (K4)

Self-assessment questions

The following questions have been designed to enable you to assess your current knowledge of this topic. The answers are provided on page 61.

Question SA1

Which of the following is most likely to be found in a review of a functional specification?

A. Undefined boundary values

B. Unreachable code

C. A failure in the system

D. A memory leak

Question SA2

Which of the following has learning as one of its main purposes?

A. Walkthrough

B. Informal review

C. Technical review

D. Inspection

Question SA3

Which of the following always makes use of entry and exit criteria?

A. Walkthrough

B. Informal review

      C. Technical review

      D. Inspection

PRINCIPLES OF REVIEWS

The review process

The Foundation syllabus focused attention on two aspects of the review process: phases for a formal review, and roles and responsibilities. In this chapter we will take a practical approach to describing the nature of the review process and the characteristics that make reviews an effective way to test work products.

Whatever review type we select it is always helpful to have a basic framework to guide us. Here are some of the main drivers for a successful review activity:

Planning

All reviews should be planned so that the time and resources required are recognised and scheduled. This does not preclude, say, a designer deciding to hold a walkthrough to brief the development team, but in these circumstances the availability of reviewers is not guaranteed and this would be an activity that adds to the planned reviews rather than replacing them.

Preparation

Some review types require more preparation than others, but it is generally good practice to prepare for a review carefully, giving appropriate time to careful reading, comparison of source and product documents, and reflection on the purpose of the review. In an impromptu walkthrough preparation may not be considered either necessary or helpful, but in most circumstances reviews will be more effective if the participants have prepared carefully. Setting clear objectives for any review is important in helping participants to prepare properly.

Review meeting

Review meetings may be held in either a formal or informal setting. A key success factor in a review meeting is to create a positive atmosphere, one in which an author can feel supported rather than criticised. In addition, the reviewers may then be more inclined to take ownership of the quality of the outcome and thus participate more fully in the activity.

This is not always easy to achieve and depends on the maturity of the participants, but it can be supported by positive chairing. A meeting, even an informal one, should have a set of rules about conduct and the nominated moderator should enforce those rules impartially and rigorously. Keeping the meeting moving, avoiding unhelpful diversions, clarifying points and looking for opportunities to defuse any tension are all valuable contributions from a moderator.

Rework and follow-up

The most important thing in terms of follow-up is to ensure that actions identified are completed to an agreed timetable. Setting realistic deadlines is important, but following this up to ensure that rework is completed and, if necessary, reviewed is essential. Even for the least formal reviews making sure that rework is satisfactorily completed is an effective way of ensuring that the review yields real value, thus encouraging participants to take part in future reviews.

All of these steps rely on the existence of a supportive culture. Building an appropriate climate, in which reviewers are motivated, authors are supported, rework is completed and quality improves is a key aspect of managing reviews.

Objectives and roles

All reviews need clearly defined objectives. Whatever level of formality is applied to a review its purpose must be clear to all participants so that they know what contribution is needed from them.

If we set an objective, for example, of ensuring that a set of requirements is testable then we have guided the participants in the expected outcome of their preparation. If, on the other hand, we simply set the objective of reviewing requirements we should not be surprised if reviewers point out grammatical and spelling errors and air their own views about what should be in a requirement rather than the intended (but unstated) objective of the review. The setting of clear objectives is key to a focused and effective review.

Roles are of two kinds: there is the role played in making the review happen and there is the role used to provide a technical perspective on the document being reviewed. Roles needed to make a review happen include the manager who schedules the reviews and ensures resources are made available, the chair (moderator) who ensures the meeting runs smoothly, the reviewers themselves, the author, and possibly a scribe to capture agreed defects and rework actions. Technical roles include tester, developer, business analyst and user. These all serve to provide a view on the document from perspectives matching the development life cycle. Checklists can be useful in guiding reviewers on typical defects to look out for, based on previous projects.

Inputs and outcomes

Reviews are conducted on work products. The inputs to a review should include the source documents (i.e. the documents used to create the work product). If a review is carried out to ensure that a specification adheres to a standard then the standard needs to be an input; if a review is checking one work product against an earlier work product (say a design document against a specification) then the earlier work product needs to be an input.

The source documents are important during preparation when reviewers spend time studying the relevant documents. The absence of these may mean that the review is limited to spelling and grammatical checks, or just individual opinions.

Outcomes from a review are to accept as is, to reject outright, or to accept subject to agreed modifications being made.

CHECK OF UNDERSTANDING CU1

1. List the steps required in a review process.
2. Explain the value of setting clear objectives at the start of a review.
3. List three roles in a formal review
4. List three potential outcomes of a review

TYPES OF REVIEW

There are many types of review. IEEE Standard 1028-1997 defines some review types that are used in organisations around the world, but the types may be implemented differently in different places or organisations may choose to modify the 'standard' type for their own particular purposes.

In this chapter we provide a brief outline of some of the review types defined in IEEE 1028-1997 as a framework for understanding the differences between review types and a basis for implementation of reviews. The main purpose is to put the alternative types into perspective rather than to explain them in detail, but the details can be found in IEEE 1028-1997 if you want to follow up any specific points.

Walkthrough

Walkthroughs are held to identify defects, improve products and educate staff. The IEEE 1028-1997 approach is relatively formal, involving distribution of documents, a preparation period and an overview presentation by the walkthrough leader. At the other end of the spectrum walkthroughs may be conducted in an ad hoc way by gathering together an appropriate group of people and 'walking through' a work product, so that participants can gain a general impression of the document, raise questions and identify any potential defects.

A key purpose of a walkthrough is education. This can be of various kinds, including familiarising a team with the principles behind a new design, enabling new staff to acquire a working knowledge of a system that is undergoing modification, or preparing users to take part in an acceptance test. In each case the clear identification of objectives is vitally important.

Walkthroughs can be used as part of a progressive review approach as outlined in *Review selection and deployment* on page 53.

EXERCISE 1 – WALKTHROUGHS

A new system is being created. A form of iterative development, Agile development, is being used. The requirements capture process is typical of iterative development projects in that limited requirements are available. The functionality for the first iteration has been sketched out, but there is a real need for a quality system to be delivered, in good time.

Which of the following would provide the best reasoning for using walkthroughs on the first set of requirements?

A. They will ensure that managers understand what will be delivered for each iteration, so they can provide contingency.
B. Given the interest in quality, the requirements can be reviewed in detail, to ensure that the developers understand what is required.
C. Lessons can be learnt from the first iteration, which should help to improve on performance for subsequent iterations.
D. They will enable a wide range of stakeholders to understand what will be built and tested for the first iteration.

Technical review

Technical reviews are used mainly to evaluate work products to determine their suitability for their intended use and their conformance to specifications and standards. They will also identify any deviations from specifications and standards, so technical reviews also record defects. As well as recommending the acceptance or otherwise of a work product, a technical review may also identify what needs to be done to make the work product acceptable and provide recommendations. A technical review may consider a complete work product or limit its scope to specific aspects. For example a technical review may report on the acceptability of a requirements specification in its entirety or it may report on the testability aspects of the requirements specification.

Technical reviews are, by their nature, formal and entail careful preparation by the participants. To this end the review team members are selected and briefed well in advance of the review and documentation is distributed sufficiently early to allow time for quality reviews together with a timetable for return of comments and for forwarding these to the author for consideration before the review meeting. At the meeting defects would be agreed and documented, and a list prepared for the review leader to prioritise and pass to the author. A recommendation to accept, rework or reject the work product would also be prepared.

EXERCISE 2 – TECHNICAL REVIEWS

The system outlined in Exercise 1 on page 49 is being built.

The first iteration has been successfully delivered. It concentrated on the look and feel of the system. The next iterations will focus on the functionality required for the middle- and back-end systems. One of the developers has expressed concern about the security of the system. He has worked on a system whereby security of personal details was compromised, leading to significant embarrassment to his employers. He has suggested that this part of the system be properly defined, and has proposed a technical review of the resulting specification.

Which of the following could provide the best justification for using technical reviews in this Agile development?

A. Despite the iterative process, technical reviews should always be used on technical specifications.

B. A technical review will explain to management why there may be a slip in the delivery date.

C. A technical review will enable security vulnerabilities to be discussed in detail, and any loopholes uncovered.

D. A technical review will explain to the users where they should focus their test efforts on release of the iteration into test.

Inspection

An inspection is normally the most formal of the reviews and has many similarities with the technical review.

This is a highly developed process that focuses on:

- calibrating the level of detail in preparation, for example by specifying the required review preparation time based on document length and complexity;
- using formal rules;
- collecting data to assess both the processes by which work products are created and the inspection process itself.

These processes make inspection a statistical quality control activity as well as a review type.

The importance of process, data collection and analysis is underlined in formal training for moderators and inspectors, while the process elements help to ensure that the potential benefits of inspections can be achieved (this is paramount in the face of the significant costs of running inspections).

An early briefing meeting, for example, can ensure that individual inspectors understand the process to be used, the role they are to adopt, the rules, and the implications of setting inspection rates.

At a kick-off meeting the documents can be distributed and details of roles, inspection rates and the rules governing identification of relevant defects can be formalised as inspectors are tasked with preparation for the inspection.

The meeting may be relatively short and focus on agreeing and recording what has been found.

The data analysis and follow-up then become an important link to process improvement as well as defect correction.

As with most types of review there is much variation in the conduct of inspections, with forms emerging that are suitable for the 'documentation light' iterative processes such as Agile development. (www.agilealliance.org)

EXERCISE 3 – INSPECTIONS

It is unusual to find the full inspection process being followed routinely in iterative development projects – they are usually too costly in time and money.

Which part of the inspection process could we make use of here, to best effect?

A. Train the moderators for the technical reviews so that they can manage the process better.
B. Inspect the requirements for every other iteration to improve overall quality of the system.
C. Collect metrics at the end of each iteration on defects being found by severity and priority, and use this to plan for the next iteration.
D. Include the managers in the reviews so that they can appreciate the costs involved better and provide more contingency for things going wrong.

Management review

IEEE 1028-1997 states that the purpose of a management review is to monitor progress, determine the status of plans and schedules, confirm requirements and their system allocation, and evaluate the effectiveness of management approaches used to achieve fitness for purpose.

Examples of the kinds of work products that might be subjected to management review would be risk management plans, configuration management plans and defect reports.

Specific management decisions reviewed might include responses to defect reports or decisions to release software when completion criteria have not been met.

The main difference between management reviews and other kinds of review covered in this chapter would be the attendees, who would include management staff as well as (possibly) technical staff. Input documents will be the relevant management documents and outcomes would typically be in the form of an action plan to address any errors or weaknesses discovered.

A management review is not necessarily conducted in a single meeting. Ideally the management review activity would be a continuous review of project reports and management practice. This will ensure that evidence of any failures or any weaknesses in routine processes are identified early, so that appropriate action can be taken to resolve issues and, equally importantly, to prevent further occurrences of the same weakness. This kind of continuous management review is usually a component of a quality management system.

EXERCISE 4 – MANAGEMENT REVIEWS

Continuing with the project in Exercise 1 on page 49, we are at iteration 3. At the end of this a management review has been scheduled. You have been asked to facilitate this review.

Which of the following would be most useful at the review?

i.   Developer representatives

ii.   Business representatives

iii.   Test representatives

iv.   Project manager

v.   Copies of all requirements documentation

vi.   Copies of all defects found so far

vii.   Overtime sheets of all staff

viii.   Defect trends over the iterations

ix.   Overall costs so far

A. iv, viii and ix

B. i–iv, viii and ix

C. ii, iv, viii and ix

D. iv–ix

Informal reviews

Informal reviews are not a review type in their own right. Level of formality is determined by the existence or otherwise of processes such as defined entry and exit criteria, stipulated minimum preparation times, allocation of roles and responsibilities, dedicated review meeting, recorded metrics and follow-up. Thus an informal technical review may include preparation time, but may forego the formal meeting in favour of sending comments in by email.

The review process has become increasingly sophisticated in recent times, in the ways that reviews are defined and implemented, such as using common storage areas (e.g. Microsoft® SharePoint®) to upload comments and notify participants of a new version of a document, webinars to hold the meetings and drop-down menus in spreadsheets to facilitate review feedback in a common format. However, there are still many organisations where reviews have never been used or where the use of reviews has been limited by cultural factors. In these organisations introducing reviews gradually, perhaps by starting with informal walkthroughs, may encourage the uptake of the more formal review types.

CHECK OF UNDERSTANDING CU2 – REVIEW TYPES

Copy and complete the table.

Comparison of review types

Characteristics	Man-agement Review	Walk-through	Technical Review	Inspection
Purpose				
Attendees				
Leadership				
Data recorded				
Reviewer roles				

Review selection and deployment

Practical review selection and deployment will depend on a complex interplay of factors such as:

- The development life cycle in use – a sequential life cycle can use reviews at each test level while an iterative life cycle will need to incorporate any reviews within timeboxes.
- Skill and experience of development and testing staff – reviews can be only as good as the staff are capable of making them.
- Review culture – a well-entrenched review culture will be supportive; early attempts at reviews may attract some hostility and negative attitudes.

Specific review types may be used in isolation but it is common to identify an effective strategy that uses a combination of review types and dynamic testing to achieve an overall quality target. Reviews can be expected to identify defects in specifications and source code, while dynamic testing will detect defects that are visible when software is executed.

A combination of reviews can provide progressive confidence. For example, a major requirements document may be reviewed several times:

- Very early in development – a walkthrough of the main structure may be useful to invite critical comment and to educate team members on the approach.
- At a first draft stage – a further walkthrough could be used to identify and remove significant defects.

- At a second draft stage – a technical review could be used to determine the document's readiness for use and recommend any improvements necessary.
- Finally, an inspection might be appropriate to identify if the work product is ready for release to the next stage.

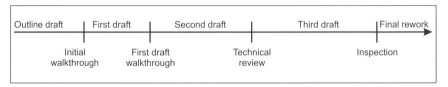

FIGURE 2.1   *Progressive reviews*

Other combinations can be substituted in different circumstances. For example, in an organisation not used to reviews the early review activity might be confined to walkthroughs but with increasing levels of documentation and formality of process. As experience and confidence grow checklists can be introduced to capture lessons learned from early experience and ensure that they are applied to future reviews.

Where life cycles do not routinely generate detailed specification documents (e.g. in an iterative life cycle), a lighter style of reviews might be appropriate in which the review process matches the timeboxed development steps.

PERFORMING SUCCESSFUL REVIEWS

This section provides some guidance on the practical performance of reviews to guide candidates in meeting the requirements of the Intermediate syllabus to have conducted a review.

One important thing to remember is that making time for reviews can be difficult for participants because they often have to fit in preparation within their normal work schedule. Anything that can be done to minimise the disruption and encourage careful preparation is worth doing (such as making quiet rooms available).

Preparing for reviews

Reviews are much more effective if participants are properly prepared. This means, ideally, that they should have had some basic training in review techniques. Whether or not training has been given there are several things that participants need to know, such as:

- What is appropriate behaviour in a review? How do I offer criticism of a document without appearing to criticise the author? How do I receive criticism of my work without feeling personally attacked? The difference between a critical review (reviewing something against a standard of some kind and reporting on the differences) and criticism in its popular use (finding fault in a negative way) needs to be understood and appreciated by everyone involved in any kind of review.

- What is the purpose of the review? What will be gained by holding the review?
- What perspective am I expected to reflect in the review?

Participants are likely to be more effective if they clearly understand what is expected of them and they have confidence in the way the process is being managed.

Setting up a review

Two things are important at this stage: getting participants to commit to the meeting and getting them to do the necessary preparation. The organisational culture needs to be one that encourages prompt response to invitations to meetings. This will ensure that any obstacles to the review are identified quickly and not left until the last moment. Problems at a late stage, when most participants have completed their preparation, will have a negative effect on the review and on the morale of those who participate. Busy staff might be tempted to opt out late next time if they see that this is acceptable.

The invitation is therefore an important document, physical or electronic, that signals its significance and asks for an immediate response. A positive response to the invitation must be a firm commitment, one that is locked into diaries to ensure that the review meeting will be fully attended. It is important to remember that review meetings, especially when the cost of preparation has been taken into account, are very expensive. If any invited attendees are unable to attend the meeting and they report this immediately they receive their invitation alternative participants can be found and the meeting need not be disrupted.

Attached to the invitation should be any supporting documentation needed for the review, including any checklists, and a form for the reviewer to return comments to the author. Getting comments back in good time is very important, so a reminder of this at the time of the invitation and, if necessary, at intervals leading up to the deadline, is worthwhile.

By the time of the scheduled review meeting the majority of comments should have been received, collated and reviewed by the author. This will provide focus for the review and enable the review leader to prepare a rough agenda to allocate time during the meeting.

Conducting a review

The two most important challenges to conducting an effective review are both about behaviour and both rely on effective leadership from the review leader.

The first challenge is about ensuring appropriate behaviour. This requires constant monitoring of the discussion for signs of personal comments, inappropriate remarks, or anything that causes or increases tension. If these kinds of problems arise they should be dealt with by steering the discussion away from the sensitive areas and, if necessary, reminding participants about acceptable behaviour in a review.

The second challenge is ensuring that the review achieves its objectives by avoiding digressions and time wasting. The most significant digression likely to arise is the tendency to try to solve problems identified at the review. While it can be very satisfying to identify a solution there and then there is a real risk that the conversation about solutions will not be resolved quickly or that it will identify a simple but spurious solution: it is better to identify and record the problems and leave solutions until after the review.

At the end of a review it is also important to agree the defects found and actions planned and to ensure that these are documented, so time should be set aside to close the review in an orderly way and ensure everyone knows what is expected of them at the follow-up stage.

Following up a review

The main activity in follow-up is usually with the author, who will be making any necessary and agreed changes. This may need support from others, and the review leader should monitor progress and be ready to offer help and support if necessary. A review of the reworked material may be necessary, even if that had not been expected at the time of the first review, and the review leader will need to be ready to arrange this.

Clear and simple reporting of defects and actions helps by simplifying follow-up and may also provide valuable data on the performance of the review and the quality of the reviewed work product. Table 2.1 provides a simple example of the kind of data that can easily be gathered from any review; over time data in this form will point to any significant anomalies in the work products being reviewed and may reveal trends in quality of work products and of reviews.

TABLE 2.1   *Review reporting form*

	Defects					
	Major			Minor		
Type of Defect	Missing	Wrong	Extra	Missing	Wrong	Extra
Standards violation	-	5	-	4	10	-
Misuse of terms	-	4	-	3	8	-
Diagramming conventions	-	-	-	-	-	-
Requirements consistency	1	1	2	-	-	2
. . . . . .						
. . . . . .						
Totals	1	10	2	7	18	2

Table 2.1 lists types of defect that have emerged as significant over a period. Standards violations, in this case, have been the most prevalent cause of defects in reviewed documents, followed by misuse of terms and so on. Defects are counted from the review defects that are being reworked after the review and categorised as major (a defect likely to lead to failure of a software product if not corrected) or minor (a defect likely to make support more difficult, for example). Further subcategorisations identify whether the defect was an omission (e.g. a specification that does not address one or more requirements), something that is wrong (e.g. a diagramming notation used incorrectly) or something that has been inappropriately added (e.g. a function included in a specification but not derived from requirements). The totals by row and column in a table indicate which types of defect are most prevalent so that these can be addressed with appropriate priority, and what categories of defect are most common. A tendency to add functionality to specifications that exceeds the requirements, for example, is worth investigating. There could be a number of possible root causes: weak requirements that need to be made more complete; poor discipline in managing requirements through development; or enthusiastic developers who would benefit from a little guidance on the importance of requirements traceability through development to testing. A simple table such as this is very easy and inexpensive to produce at the end of each review and provides data from which process improvements could be made across an organisation.

Assessing the effectiveness of a review

What determines the effectiveness of a review? The outcome is the best measure of success, but the way the review is conducted will have an impact on performance and should also be monitored.

Monitoring the way reviews are performed is relatively easy and can be both enjoyable and instructive for all those involved. The following exercise suggests an approach that can be used as a basis for training and assessing review effectiveness.

EXERCISE 5 – REVIEW ASSESSMENT

Here is a simple exercise that will help to develop a positive review culture.

Select a document that can be reviewed in no more than two hours, that is a fairly short (say 10 pages) and simple document, and set up a review.

At the review meeting record the discussion. An audio recording is better than nothing but a video recording is vastly superior. After the meeting listen to or watch the recording to see how well you did, looking for any clues in verbal language, volume of exchanges or body language, of tensions in the group. Rate your success in identifying defects and in not alienating the author.

> After about 3 or 4 weeks repeat the exercise and see how much you have improved. If you need to, repeat it again after 4–6 weeks to ensure the lessons are entrenched and the culture is building.
>
> To make the exercise even more effective use a facilitator to set up the review and record it. The facilitator can then focus attention on the key lessons to be learned and direct participants to the most interesting parts of the recording.

Determining effectiveness by results is a more difficult exercise, but monitoring review outputs offers many other benefits. The basic question is about the impact that reviews should have. On one hand, as review performance improves we should expect to identify more defects in work products; on the other hand the detection and removal of defects in work products should result in a gradual improvement in the quality of work products produced. Which of these predominates will depend on whether the review culture or the process improvement culture is the more effective, but monitoring results in a form such as that in Table 2.1 will provide some useful trend information. Based on this, more sophisticated reporting and monitoring could be developed to enable effectiveness to be assessed in greater detail.

Using the assessment to improve review performance

Review performance can be improved in two ways: first, and most simply, by correcting any issues raised about reviews as they are conducted; secondly, by acting on recorded data about the reviews. This could lead into process improvements in a number of areas and it is important to continue to collect the same data to reflect the changes you make to improve the culture and the process. You may decide that more sophisticated data is required to identify more detail of process weaknesses but do not abandon the simple data until you can see that any improvements are yielding the right kind of trends in that data.

SUMMARY

This chapter has reviewed the material on reviews from the Foundation syllabus and extended it by providing more detail of how the basic principles can be applied in a practical situation. The review types from Foundation have also been reviewed and one new review type, the management review, has been added and described.

The most significant new material is in the sections on how to select and deploy appropriate types of review in practical situations and on the practical implementation of reviews. An exercise has been included to encourage the use of reviews and some reflection on how to make them as effective as possible.

A mind map of the key topics in this chapter is in Appendix A.

EXAMPLE EXAMINATION QUESTIONS

Scenario 1

A major supermarket is upgrading its online store in response to recent changes in consumer spending. It has reduced its 'premium' products range by offering less organic meat and vegetables and less exotic fruit and vegetables. It has increased its 'friendly' product range by increasing its locally sourced produce, and its 'fair-trade' range by including more products from overseas where growers are assured a fair price for their products.

The front-end design is changing to allow customers to select their shopper preferences, which are:

- environmentally friendly;
- family friendly;
- fair to all.

Customers will then be offered products falling into each of these categories.

The changes to the front end are considered to be simple, when compared with the changes required to the back end, to provide each customer group with the correct product choices.

The development life cycle is Agile development. One of the developers has begun creating a high-level design to help clarify the product categories.

He has decided to hold a review of the high-level design.

E1

Which one of the following review types would be suitable for the high-level design, for the reasoning given?

A. A walkthrough of the design, so that those building the front end can understand how their software will interact with the back end.

B. A technical review of the design so that each product category can be tightly defined before the functionality is built.

C. An inspection of the design to see if it can be easily reused for later iterations.

D. A management review of the design to ensure that it will be fit for purpose.

E2

For which of the following reasons would a management review be suitable?

A. It will enable the front-end design to be updated throughout the iterations in line with information from the marketing manager.

B. It will enable the most technical aspects of the system to be properly documented.

C. It will enable the way defects are prioritised for fixing to be assessed.

D. It will ensure that each developer understands their priorities for each build.

Scenario 2

A company, MCB, sells a system to monitor the cabin pressure of aircraft in flight to major passenger aircraft manufacturers.

When the pressure is at levels considered unsafe for passengers, a triggering mechanism is used to deploy oxygen masks. Each manufacturer customises MCB's product to work with their on-board mask triggering system.

There have been recent reports by cabin staff on one particular manufacturer's aircraft type (FlyMe) that the masks are being deployed (incorrectly) for minor changes in cabin pressure. This is causing undue stress to passengers and cabin staff alike.

The problem has been investigated, but at this stage it is unknown whether the problem is across all aircraft or limited to just the one reported.

FlyMe has called a meeting with MCB's staff. In order to prepare for the meeting, the managers of MCB have decided that a technical review should be conducted.

E3

Which of the following would you subject to a technical review at this time?

A. The functional specification for the mechanism for deployment of the masks.

B. The functional specification for the monitoring of cabin pressure.

C. The functional specification for customisations of the system from FlyMe.

D. The code for FlyMe's customisations.

E4

MCB uses inspections as one of its key review types. The management team is revisiting this process. It uses the V model for development.

Which of the following benefits would be expected from inspections at MCB?

i. The quality of the pressure monitoring code would be improved.

ii. The time taken for the customisations by the aircraft manufacturers would be reduced.

iii. The time taken for subsequent changes to the pressure monitoring system would be reduced.

iv. The defect turnaround times would be reduced.

v. The management will have better visibility of time taken to build each product.

A. i and iii
B. ii and iii
C. ii and iv
D. iv and v

ANSWERS TO SELF-ASSESSMENT QUESTIONS (ON PAGES 45)

SA1. A
SA2. A
SA3. D

ANSWERS TO CHECKS OF UNDERSTANDING

CU1 (on page 48)

1. Steps required in a review process include:
    - review planning;
    - review preparation;
    - review conduct;
    - rework and follow-up.
2. The value of setting clear objectives at the start of a review is that the review is more likely to be focused on what is important and required, and efficiency should increase as a result.
3. Roles in a formal review include:
    - chair (moderator);
    - reviewers;
    - author;
    - scribe.

    Note that the manager role is not active in the actual review. The role is required to provide budget and schedule for conducting reviews.
4. Three potential outcomes of a review are:
    - to accept the document as it is;
    - to reject the document;
    - to accept the document with actions to be followed up.

CU2 (on page 53)

Characteristics	Management review	Walkthrough	Technical review	Inspection
Purpose	To monitor consistency of management actions with defined procedures.	To aid understanding of a document, find defects.	To evaluate a work product's suitability for intended use.	Defect finding, process improvement.
Attendees	Management, technical staff where appropriate.	Any interested (and invited) stakeholder.	Technical staff	Those with clearly defined roles (tester, developer, analyst etc.).
Leadership	Management	Author of the document.	Chair (moderator)	Trained moderator
Data recorded	Record of errors and planned actions.	List of errors or marked-up document.	List of errors, associated actions and unresolved issues.	Data related to source document (e.g. size of document); errors identified at the inspection; data related to the inspection (e.g. inspection rates).
Reviewer Roles	Includes the key decision maker.	Author, attendee	Chair, scribe, author, reviewer	Moderator, scribe, author, reviewer

ANSWERS TO EXERCISES

Exercise 1 (on page 49)

The best answer is D. Here is the reasoning.

Answer A: The first part is applicable – a walkthrough will facilitate understanding. However, the second part suggests that the walkthrough will enable the provision of contingency. This is unlikely to be the outcome of a walkthrough, a decision on the provision of adequate contingency will require a more thorough approach, such as a risk assessment exercise. (There is more on this in Chapter 3.)

Answer B: The first part suggests that requirements will be reviewed in detail in a walkthrough. This is unlikely.

Answer C: Lessons can be learnt from a project which is ongoing. The scenario states that we are at the start of the project. In addition, we are conducting a walkthrough of the requirements, not progress to date.

Exercise 2 (on page 50)

The best answer is C. Here is the reasoning.

Answer A: While a technical review is usually useful, we cannot say that we should always conduct one. They are costly and their use must be justifiable in terms of risk and cost to remedy any defects found.

Answer B: A technical review focuses on the technical aspects of the project, not project timescales or budgets.

Answer D would be more appropriate in a walkthrough.

Exercise 3 (on page 51)

The best answer is A. Here is the reasoning.

Answer B: Since this is an Agile environment, functionality agreed for one iteration may be changed in the next, thus ensuring accuracy of one set of requirements is unlikely to yield a good return. Also, the requirements are unlikely to be detailed or stable enough to warrant the cost of an inspection.

Answer C: Collection of information defects found should be carried out throughout the testing, not at the end of the iteration. Assuming that the requirements will change for the next iteration, metrics on incidents from the previous iteration may not be wholly applicable.

Answer D: A manager's inclusion in an inspection of a technical document should be from a technical perspective (should they possess the required knowledge), not costs (these will of course need to be considered, but not in this process).

Exercise 4 (on page 52)

The best answer is B. Here is the reasoning.

Option i.   Developer representatives – yes, these are stakeholders.

Option ii.   Business representatives – as option i.

Option iii.   Test representatives – as option i.

Option iv.   Project manager – as option i.

Option v.   Copies of all requirements documentation – a summary would be more useful.

Option vi.   Copies of all defects found so far – as option v.

Option vii.   Overtime sheets of all staff – as option v.

Option viii.   Defect trends over the iterations – this is key.

Option ix.   Overall costs so far – this may be important, so should be included.

This leads to options i–iv, viii and ix being the most appropriate.

ANSWERS TO EXAMPLE EXAMINATION QUESTIONS

E1 (on page 59)

The correct answer is A.

Answer B is incorrect because a technical review is very likely to result in a tightly defined design. This project is following an Agile life cycle, however, where the design can be expected to change.

Using inspections, as answer C suggests, is again unlikely to be of much benefit on a design that is expected to evolve as the project progresses.

Answer D, a management review, will not include review of a design. It may review the design *process*, but not the actual design.

E2 (on page 59)

The correct answer is C.

Answer A refers to making design changes after input from a stakeholder – the marketing manager. While this is a likely scenario, it will not be the outcome of a management review.

Answer B, documenting the technical aspects of a system, may result from a technical review, not a management review.

Answer D, understanding priorities for each build, could result from management input, but will be part of test planning, not the result of a management review (this would review the decision-making process, not the actual decisions).

E3 (on page 60)

The correct answer is B.

Answer A is incorrect because it refers to the functional specification for mask deployment. Mask deployment is carried out by its customers, not MCB.

Answer C is incorrect because it refers to the customisations. These once again, are carried by the customers, not MCB.

Answer D is incorrect because the code for the customisations will not be MCB's responsibility.

Note that at some point the customised software and integration with mask deployment will need to be considered. However, this question is focused around MCB's software before a meeting with its customer, Flyme.

E4 (on page 60)

The correct answer is A.

Option ii is incorrect because inspections at MCB are unlikely to affect the time taken for its customers to carry out their customisations.

Option iv is incorrect because defect turnaround times are not dependent on quality of the specification. They are dependent on developer schedules and priorities.

Option v is incorrect because inspections will not allow visibility of time taken to build a product. They will allow visibility of the quality of the documents being used for each build.

3 Testing and risk

BACKGROUND

Risk, as we learned at Foundation level, is about what happens when an unwanted event occurs. The event has some probability associated with it and what happens has some negative consequences. For example, if we want a fine day for a picnic and the weather forecast tells us there is a 10 per cent chance of rain in our area then the success of our picnic is threatened and we must decide how to react to that risk. Rain is the unwanted event, 10 per cent is the probability of it occurring and a wet picnic is the potential consequence. We might then take the view that a forecasted 10 per cent chance of rain makes it highly improbable and just go ahead, choosing to ignore the risk; we might decide to take a large umbrella in case we have a shower, thus mitigating the impact of the rain; we might be pessimistic and decide to postpone the picnic until we get a more favourable weather forecast, avoiding the risk. Which choice we make will depend on a number of factors: how important is the picnic, how much would rain affect our plans, how disappointed will the picnic party be if it is postponed.

In this fairly trivial example we took account of only a single risk but we have worked through the complete risk management cycle: we identified rain as a risk; we analysed the risk (or rather the weather forecaster analysed it for us); and we decided what to do about mitigating the impact of the risk. These are the basic elements of risk management.

One of the key objectives of software testing is to reduce the risks associated with developing and using software to an acceptable level. What constitutes an acceptable level of risk will depend on the kind of software application being considered and the context in which it will be used, so risk management always calls for judgement and must always take into account the views of all the stakeholders involved.

The basic discipline for identifying and analysing risks, and for deciding on an appropriate risk mitigation strategy was addressed at Foundation level, as was the risk-based testing approach. At the Intermediate level we focus on the analysis of scenarios to differentiate between different types of risk, and the selection of the most appropriate course of action, based on our analysis.

INTRODUCTION TO TESTING AND RISK

Learning objectives

The learning objectives for this chapter are listed below. You can confirm that you have achieved these by using the self-assessment questions on page 67, the 'Check of understanding' boxes distributed through the text, and the example examination questions at the end of the chapter. The chapter summary will remind you of the key ideas.

We have given a K number to each topic to represent the level of understanding required for that topic; for an explanation of the K numbers see Chapter 6 and Appendix B.

Review of Foundation Certificate content

- Review the main principles and themes from relevant areas of the Foundation syllabus, all of which are considered part of the required knowledge for this syllabus. (K1)

Introduction to risk

- Recall the nature of product risk and project risk and their effects. (K1)
- Explain how risks can interact with other risks. (K2)
- Describe typical risks associated with given application domains. (K2)

Risk management

- Recall the core activities of risk management: risk identification, risk analysis and risk mitigation, and explain the importance of achieving maximum stakeholder involvement in these activities. (K2)
- Explain the relationship between risk and testing. (K2)

Product risk identification and analysis

- Identify typical product risks. (K2)
- Analyse a situation and recognise risks within that scenario. (K4)

Self-assessment questions

The following questions have been designed to enable you to check your current level of understanding of the topics in this chapter. The answers are on page 82.

Question SA1

Which of the following provides the best definition of a product risk?

A. The system may not be delivered on time.

B. Testers may not be available to test the system at the required times.

C. A feature may not work as expected.

D. The product may not sell as well as expected.

Question SA2

In which document would specific product risks first be considered?

A. Test strategy

B. Test specification

C. Test procedure

D. Test policy

Question SA3

In which order should a risk management exercise be conducted?

i.   Analyse risks to determine likelihood and impact.

ii. Mitigate risks by conducting testing where possible.

iii. Identify risks.

iv. Gather stakeholders together.

A. i, iii, iv, ii

B. iii, i, ii, iv

C. iv, iii, i, ii

D. iii, iv, i, ii

RISK FUNDAMENTALS

Categories of risk

As we saw at the beginning of this chapter, risk is a feature of life that we handle every day.

When we take on a major activity such as building a software product our awareness of risk is heightened significantly, partly because the risks we face are not the familiar everyday variety, partly because the negative outcomes associated with risk are not always obvious, and partly because the mechanisms for avoiding risk are less obvious and not part of the everyday pattern of life. However, there is an infrastructure in place to help us, in the form of software engineering disciplines, project management methodologies, education and training and so on.

Our main problem, though, is predicting the likely risk events for our specific projects and problem domains, and understanding whether the infrastructure we have is adequate to protect us from the risks that arise.

We begin by looking at the main types of risk that can arise in software development projects.

Safety risks

A risk in this category is one which, if it materialises, may cause harm to an individual. For these types of risk cost of mitigation is seldom an issue.

Safety critical systems include many in the management, delivery and support of road, rail, sea and air transport systems, defence systems, pharmaceutical and medical systems.

Economic risks

An economic risk is defined as one which, if it occurs, could cause financial loss to the company.

This could include a project that has been delivered on time and to budget, but does not yield the benefits expected and budgeted for by the company, such as cost savings, productivity improvements or increased revenues.

It could include a project that has cost more than was budgeted for, leading to late delivery of the system or cancellation of the project altogether, with no mechanism for recovery of project spend by the company, thus causing an economic loss to the company and loss of any anticipated economic benefits the system was intended to deliver.

Another example includes systems needed to meet legislative requirements, such as the Sarbanes–Oxley legislations in the financial services sector. The cost of implementation has been reported to have had a negative effect on small firms (notably those outside the USA), whose revenues did not increase sufficiently to cover the cost of compliance.

Security risks

A security risk is one where access to a system may be compromised, allowing those without legitimate intentions to access, manipulate and use the data held on the system.

Any software application that is web-based, for example, is likely to be under attack at some time. The technology of security threats is changing continuously, so the nature of any attack is hard to predict, but basic security can always be built into any product at a cost. The nature of security risks is such that the real judgement is about the level of security required and the cost of achieving that level.

Political risks

Political risks arise when political influences affect the outcome of a project, such as the risk of a political party coming to power and changing something that affects the market for a product or the general climate within which a proposed product will operate (generating an economic risk). On a more local level, a change in a management team that involves a change in project sponsor or a change in business strategy that makes a proposed product less attractive.

Technical risks

Technical risks are those that arise from the technology being used to construct a product. This may be related to new approaches to development, such as a first Agile project, or the use of untried technology, such as hosting an existing product on a new platform, an example of which would be upgrading a PC platform from Windows® XP to Windows® Vista.

Product risks and project risks

Product risks and project risks are differentiated primarily because we deal with them differently.

Product risk is the risk that the product we are building will not meet the purpose for which it is being built. This might be because the original design was flawed or the features have not been properly coded.

Examples might include an air traffic control incident caused by a software malfunction, a banking system mishandling customer accounts, and a government system making confidential information public.

A project risk is one where the project timescales, budget and resources may be compromised. The project may overrun and deliver late; it may overrun on budget so that the project costs more than expected; project staff may lack the required skills; or there may not be enough of them.

Note that product risks can lead to project risks and vice versa. A poorly performing product may require more bug fixes and retesting than expected, leading to increased project costs. Conversely, not having the right skill sets may lead to a poorly functioning product.

Note also that a project risk is distinct from an economic risk. The former is specific to a particular project (such as project X should cost £1.5 million, but may cost £2 million). The latter is applicable to the organisation as a whole (such as the revenues from successful delivery of project X are expected to be £10 million, but may be less if the product does not sell well). Note that a project risk could lead to an economic risk (e.g. if project X above does cost the extra £0.5 million), if the loss cannot be recovered by the company.

CHECK OF UNDERSTANDING CU1 – RISK CATEGORIES

1. List four different categories of risk.
2. Explain the difference between an economic risk and a project risk.

EXERCISE 1 – PRODUCT RISKS

An incident management tool is being upgraded to allow an email notification to be sent to the developer to whom it has been assigned, once it has been accepted, and the priority rating assigned.

Which of the following is a product risk?

A. The developers may receive too many requests for bug fixes.
B. Testers may assign higher priority ratings than necessary to ensure that their bugs are fixed first.
C. Emails may not be received in good time by the developers.
D. The upgrade to the email servers may take longer than expected.

EXERCISE 2 – PROJECT RISKS

A new product is being created to allow householders to measure their overall home energy consumption on a daily basis. This will be done by fitting a unit into the house. The budget for development is £750k. Sales projections show a first-year income of £300k, growing to £500k per annum over a three-year period. The launch date is planned for 1 October to coincide with the start of the winter season.

Which of the following are project risks?

i.   The first year income may be less than £300k.

ii.   Development may cost more than £750k.

iii. The product may not be ready in time for the launch date.

iv.   Householders may think that the units are too large for their homes.

A. i and ii
B. ii and iii
C. iii and iv
D. i and iv

TESTING AND RISK

Product risks in software development are usually mitigated through testing. Testing can identify the defects that contribute to product risk; contribute to risk mitigation by demonstrating that defects leading to risk have been successfully removed; quantify risk remaining at any stage in a project; and contribute to release decisions by identifying what needs to be done to achieve an acceptable level of risk.

Project risks are the province of project managers but testing, as a major part of any software development project, will contribute to the information provided in order to assess the levels of risk to a project.

Causes of risk

Risk and application domains

Here we pick up on the application domains discussed in Chapter 1. There were four: stand-alone PC-based, mainframe, client–server and web-based.

Applications residing on a stand-alone machine carry the risks associated with dependence on a set of resources held on the host machine (for example a PC). As you saw earlier, this could include the system requirements in terms of memory and speed, as well as compatibility with the operating system.

In the mainframe domain, risks surround the ability of the computer to store and process data reliably and efficiently. Thus data integrity, robustness, performance, security and recovery (including fail-over) are key testing concerns for this application domain.

In the client–server domain, risks surround the ability of the server to process data, as required by its clients. Thus testing for concurrency and throughput of data are key concerns in testing.

In a web-based application, risks surround making the application available to the world at large. These include the risk of poor performance, poor security and compatibility with different web browsers.

These examples illustrate the need to consider carefully the risks associated with a given application domain and to take these into account in developing a testing strategy.

Risk and life cycles

Here we look at risks surrounding the use of the two major software development life cycles: the V model and iterative development.

In the V life cycle, a key risk is that requirements agreed to at the start of development may have changed by the time the system has been released. If we imagine that we have a project following the V model and each activity will last one month, then we may have a nine-month project. In following the V model, we would write the tests for acceptance testing in month 1, but run them in month 9. If the tests fail, we would know this very late in the life cycle (at the very end of the development life cycle) and this will create a product risk. In reality, although changes to requirements are usually fed back through the system, as change requests. However, this could mean that tests designed at the start are not run in their original form, leading to a need for rework, thus increasing costs (a project risk).

In iterative development, the key risks centre on the changing requirements. The requirements may be limited to simple use cases initially. The lack of detailed requirements documentation could limit systematic testing (e.g. the use of specification-based techniques) leading to product risk. The changing requirements will necessitate significant regression testing; if this becomes more extensive than was expected project costs will increase and delivery dates may be threatened (project risks).

Iterative development reduces the risk that a product will not be acceptable, mainly by involving users at every stage, but the approach may also generate project risk if testing is limited.

Risk and development approaches

The development approaches previously discussed were reusing software and use of commercial off-the-shelf (COTS) software.

When reusing software, a key risk is that the reused component may not work as expected when integrated into a new system.

When using COTS systems, the risks surround the functionality of the system in its new environment. When customising the software, the risks include the functionality of the newly created software when integrated with the original package, as well as liability when things go wrong. If the buyer has made the changes, then the vendor may claim that any defects found are due to the changes made.

Risk and project management

When considering risks to a project, it is worth remembering that dealing with them inevitably entails costs, which may be higher than budgeted for. It is for this reason that risk assessment exercises should be carried out as early as possible (and before budgets are set), to reduce the risk of insufficient funds being allocated to a project.

In the real world, however, limited budget in testing for IT projects is not uncommon. This could result in increased product risk, where insufficient testing could result in poor functionality not being discovered before release of the system.

CHECK OF UNDERSTANDING CU2 – CAUSES OF RISK

Redraw the table to match each risk description to where it is most associated.

Risk	Association
Late delivery of requirements	Development approach
Insufficient budget	Application domain
Reused software not working as expected	Project management
Poor security	Development life cycle

RISK MANAGEMENT

The risk management process

The risk management process has four stages: risk identification; risk analysis; risk mitigation; and risk monitoring. In this section we will look at the first three of these stages, considering the alternative techniques and approaches available and appropriate to each stage, and how they fit together in an overall risk management strategy. In this section we will look in more detail at each stage and, in the next section, we will explain risk-based testing and its role in mitigating product risk.

Figure 3.1 shows the risk management process.

Risk identification

Risk identification is the initial step of recognising what risks are present (i.e. what unwanted events might occur). At this stage the main priority is to ensure that as many risks as possible are identified rather than analysing any of them in any depth. The emphasis is on taking the broadest possible view and involving as many different stakeholders as possible to ensure that risk is considered from many viewpoints.

Techniques for identification are those that encourage an open mind and speculation; all ideas should be welcomed and captured. Later stages of the process will analyse and quantify the risks. The following are the most commonly used identification techniques.

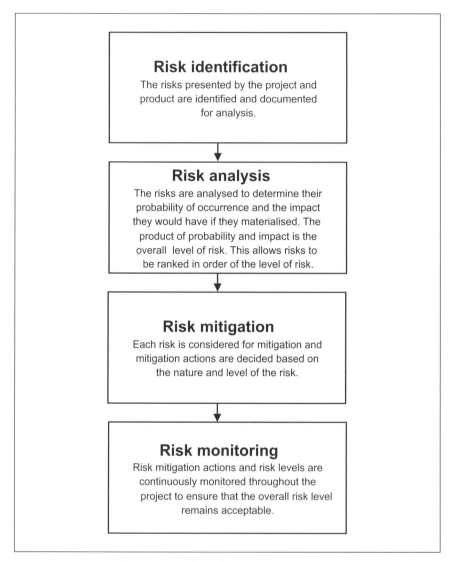

FIGURE 3.1 *The risk management process*

Brainstorming

Brainstorming is an ideal technique for capturing ideas quickly. To be really effective a brainstorm session needs to be short and intense, while participants are in a creative mood. A conducive atmosphere is vital, and participants need to feel safe from criticism or ridicule. A facilitator should be appointed to control the activity and ensure that everyone is encouraged to contribute. During the risk brainstorm session everything suggested should be recorded (ideally on a flip chart or whiteboard, but a sheet of paper would do) without comment or analysis. The session should be kept going while ideas are flowing freely, but stopped as soon as there are gaps in the flow of ideas. Often a second session, after a little break and starting from the list generated by the first brainstorm session, can yield more ideas triggered by the initial list.

Risk workshops

A workshop is a more structured session than a brainstorm session. The aim is to have as many different stakeholder viewpoints represented as possible. However, the generally accepted view is that a workshop is more effective with 8–12 participants. As for the brainstorm session, a facilitator should be appointed to run the workshop.

Lessons learned

This technique capitalises on knowledge gained from previous projects. Looking back over past projects to identify mistakes made and risks not well managed can be a powerful trigger for recognising potential risks in a current project. In this case the technique depends on the existence of some records of past projects, in the form of post-project reviews or risk registers. If a risk analysis was done for past projects and records kept, these can be useful if there are people available who were involved or who can remember the projects. This can be a good way to at least recognise risks that were not handled effectively in the past. If there are no records this is not a suitable technique, but it might be a good idea to begin keeping enough records to allow it to be used for future projects.

Interviews

Interviews are a way to ensure that all stakeholder viewpoints are considered. More structured than a brainstorm or a workshop, an interview can ensure that every viewpoint is considered and it can also ensure that every stakeholder's input is based on a consistent set of questions. An interview is inevitably more formal than a brainstorm or a workshop, and this may become an inhibiting factor; interviewees are likely to be less spontaneous and creative than in a workshop situation. Interviews can be a very good way to follow up on brainstorms or workshops to ensure that those who made little contribution are at least heard and to follow up on any questions raised by the brainstorm or workshop. The idea of workshops or brainstorming followed by interviews suggests a fairly time-consuming and expensive approach, but it will ensure that all participants have had the opportunity to contribute.

Independent assessment

Independent assessment by an expert can help to ensure that all important areas are covered, but independent experts are likely to be expensive, so this is not an approach that would normally be used except where the cost is justified, for example if an organisation is entering a safety critical area of application for the first time. Of course an independent assessment does not necessarily require an expert and there may be specialists within the organisation who are independent of the project that could carry out an effective risk assessment. This is still a relatively expensive approach, however.

Checklists and templates

Checklists and templates are both ways to provide a starting point for the risk assessment. Checklists can be based on past experience, lessons learned or input from an expert, or they can just be culled from books or produced in a brainstorm or a workshop.

Templates, typically providing the main headings for a risk assessment document, are an alternative to checklists, or they may be used to ensure that the topics included in the checklist are included in the documentation. The main thing is that everything the organisation considers important in a risk assessment is incorporated into these guidance documents. No matter how shaky the initial checklists or templates, they will improve if they are continuously updated from real project experience.

CHECK OF UNDERSTANDING CU3 – RISK IDENTIFICATION

Redraw the table to match each situation to its ideal risk identification mechanism.

Situation	Risk identification mechanism
When we have individuals with knowledge of the technical and business domains.	Brainstorm
When we have access to information from previous projects.	Risk workshops
When we do not have sufficient in-house knowledge, and have time and budget.	Lessons learned
When we have knowledge to provide a starting point of key areas to consider.	Interviews
When we want to reach consensus on areas of highest risk.	Independent assessments
When we want to gain an initial idea of potential risks.	Checklists and templates

Risk analysis

Risk analysis is about getting more information about the risks, especially the relative risk levels of the risks identified. Risk level is defined as the product of the probability of a risk occurring and the impact of the risk if it occurred. Thus if a risk had a probability of $1/100$ of occurring and its impact would be a loss to the organisation of £1,000, we would define the risk level as £10.

The aim of risk analysis is, as far as possible, to quantify the risks so that they can be ranked and prioritised. The simple example given is untypical because neither the probability of occurrence nor the impact would normally be quantifiable as precisely as in the example, if at all. Nevertheless, the definition of level of risk is still useful. If precise quantification is not possible then some more qualitative measure of probability and impact can be used. Gradings of both probability and impact could be as simple as Low, Medium or High. Figure 3.2 is an example of a matrix that can be used to record risks by level.

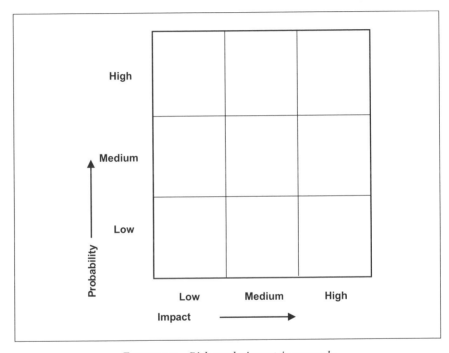

FIGURE 3.2   *Risk analysis matrix example*

If more is known, then finer grain estimates of probability and impact can be used. Instead of three levels for each there could be five, seven or even nine. The most important thing is that the matrix provides a basis for ranking risks and deciding on the priorities for risk mitigation.

Figure 3.3 provides an example of a matrix with seven levels and populates the matrix with some examples of the number of unwanted events identified in the various combinations of probability and impact. Based on a populated matrix such as this a risk mitigation strategy can be worked out.

In this example we see that the unwanted events associated with risks are spread around the matrix. A few are in the extreme corners of low impact and low probability, which can be ignored, or high impact and high probability, which demand attention. The more difficult judgements are around what to do about those that occur around the middle of the table, and here some

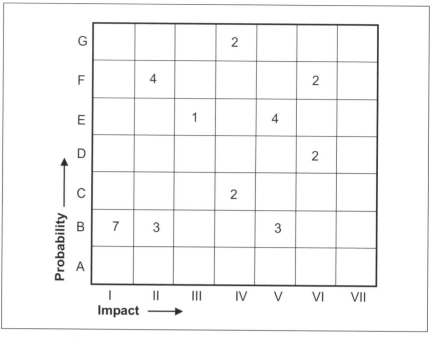

FIGURE 3.3   *Populated 7 × 7 risk analysis matrix example*

closer examination may be necessary before a risk mitigation strategy is decided.

EXERCISE 3 – RISK ANALYSIS

Consider the following risk analysis.

A.   A risk of poor load handling has been allocated a probability of low, but with a high impact.

B.   A risk of poor data integrity has been allocated a probability of medium, with high impact.

C.   A risk of poor usability has been allocated a probability of low, with low impact.

D.   A risk of poor security has a probability of low with high impact.

Create a table showing each risk, its overall risk score and the order in which it should be addressed.

Risk mitigation

Risk mitigation is the term used for the action we decide to take in tackling each risk. Mitigation actions can be anywhere on a spectrum from doing nothing at one end to doing as much as possible to eliminate the risk at the other end. In between there are many options, such as taking out insurance to cover any losses, spending extra money on specialist resources to tackle a high risk area more effectively than we could do for ourselves, or outsourcing a risky area to a third party who will take on the risk and compensate us if it materialises.

Testing is a key element of risk mitigation because it can provide evidence of the effective countering of a risk. For example, if there is a risk that a system will have inadequate performance there will need to be development action to ensure that adequate performance is achieved, and it will then be performance testing that identifies objectively whether the performance is adequate or not. For this reason the testing associated with the higher risks needs to be the priority. This is the main principle behind risk-based testing.

EXAMPLE – RISK MITIGATION STRATEGY

Let us look at potential mitigation activities for our risks identified in Exercise 3.

TABLE 3.1 *Risk mitigation strategy example*

Risk ID	Description	Mitigation
A	Poor load handling	We could use an automated tool to generate required loading to test for adequate system performance.
B	Poor data integrity	We could target testing on the data store specifically, possibly using a modelling tool (this will most likely be used by developers).
C	Poor usability	We could conduct testing based on known usability requirements. Use can be made of standardised and publicly available surveys such as SUMI and WAMMI, which are marked against a database of previous usability measurements. SUMI is the Software Usability Measurement Inventory and WAMMI stands for Website Analysis and MeasureMent Inventory. Both are based around an online questionnaire that visitors to a site fill in.
D	Poor security	We may need to engage dedicated security testing specialists depending on the type of security risks. If we need to test access permissions only, then we may be able to conduct this ourselves.

RISK-BASED TESTING

What is risk-based testing?

Risk-based testing is the term used for an approach to creating a test strategy that is based on prioritising tests by risk. The basis of the approach is a detailed risk analysis and prioritising of risks by risk level. Tests to address each risk are then specified, starting with the highest risk first.

Risk-based testing has the advantage that the most critical areas of the application are tested first, so that any delays or problems that result in testing being curtailed will not interfere with the basic principle that the most important areas of the application have been tested and risk has thereby been minimised. A risk-based approach will always seek to ensure that the areas of the application remaining untested are the least important in terms of risk at that time.

If risk-based testing is deployed with a set of exit criteria that defines acceptable risk the test manager has a sound basis for assessing remaining risk at any or every stage of testing and can always say that the work completed to date has made maximum impact on reducing risk. A set of risk-based exit criteria might include: a measure of requirements coverage, such as all requirements with priority (based on risk and value of the feature expressed by the requirement) above a certain value have been tested; some measure(s) of code or other structural coverage that gives confidence in the extent that testing has been achieved; and all defects above a certain level of criticality have been corrected and successfully retested. Criteria such as these can be tracked and reported simply, giving the test manager a quantified view of the status of testing and risk on which test summary reports can be based. In the event of testing not being complete at the planned release date a rational decision can be made about the action to be taken based on the current estimate of risk remaining. Alternative release decisions can be tested to determine the most practical.

SUMMARY

In this chapter we reviewed the material on risk from the Foundation syllabus and extended it to provide a sound basis for both overall risk management and for the creation of effective risk-based testing strategies, an area that will be further extended at the Practitioner level.

Categories of risk were identified and the nature of product and project risk were differentiated, and the tendency to mutual influence was explored in the context of risk in life cycles and in particular application domains. For testers, product risk is most open to mitigation by defining appropriate testing strategies, so we explored mechanisms for identifying, classifying and quantifying product risks.

The overall discipline of risk management is also important to testers because of the contribution testing makes as a risk reduction mechanism and we explored the overall risk management process and the significance of stakeholder involvement in the process throughout.

Finally, we introduced the approach known as risk-based testing, which will be explored in greater depth at the Practitioner level.

A mind map of the chapter content is in Appendix A.

EXAMPLE EXAMINATION QUESTIONS

Scenario

A car manufacturer (AceCars) is updating its airbag deployment system for its family cars. It has increased the number of airbags from four to nine. This has necessitated an upgrade to the airbag control software (ACS) to allow deployment of the extra airbags where appropriate.

The ACS receives information from on-board sensors. From this, it calculates the amount of deployment needed (minimal, medium and full), and from which airbag(s). For this upgrade, it will receive information from extra sensors to be used in its calculations.

AceCars employs its own in-house software development team. It uses the V model for its software development. There are four stages of testing, from unit through to factory acceptance testing.

The development team is made up of project, programming and test managers. The programmers use object-oriented methods for development.

AceCars wishes to be first to market with the extra airbags, which will allow it to increase the safety ratings for its family cars, thereby increasing sales in a very competitive market.

E1

Which of the following are risks associated with the use of the V model for this upgrade?

i. The sensors may not be responsive enough in impacts.

ii. The ACS may not be able to process the information received from the sensors quickly enough.

iii. The time required to create the high- and low-level designs may mean that insufficient time can be spent on system testing.

iv. The system may fail factory acceptance testing, necessitating costly rework.

A. i and ii

B. ii and iii

C. iii and iv

D. i and iv

E2

Which of the following is a risk associated with the development approach?

A. Information hiding may pose extra testing challenges.

B. System testing may take longer than planned.

C. The calculations may become overly complex due to the increase in the number of sensors.

D. Testers may not be able to write the factory acceptance tests at the start of development.

E3

Which of the following is a product risk of the upgrade described?

A. The extra airbags may restrict the visibility of the driver.

B. AceCars may not be awarded its desired safety rating.

C. There may be a need to use modeling tools at unit testing.

D. The ACS may not be able to process the extra sensor data quickly enough, causing incorrect deployment of the airbag(s).

ANSWERS TO SELF-ASSESSMENT QUESTIONS (ON PAGES 67–68)

SA1. C

SA2. A

SA3. C

ANSWERS TO CHECKS OF UNDERSTANDING

CU1 (on page 70)

1. Categories of risk include:
   - safety
   - economic
   - security
   - political
   - technical
   - product
   - project.

   Note we list all given in the text, not just four as required.

2. The difference between an economic risk and a project risk is that an economic risk is one which affects the company as a whole. An economic risk example is that a product, once developed and released, does not sell as well as expected, causing a loss of revenue to the company. A project risk is one that affects a project while the product is in development, such as budget and time overruns. Note that a project risk of a product costing more than predicted to build may lead to an economic risk.

CU2 (on page 73)

Here is the table reordered to show the development aspect most associated with the risk identified.

Risk	Association
Late delivery of requirements	Development life cycle
Reused software not working as expected	Development approach
Insufficient budget	Project management
Poor security	Application domain

CU3 (on page 76)

Here, we reorder the table to match the situation to its ideal risk identification mechanism.

Situation	Risk identification mechanism
When we have individuals with knowledge of the technical and business domains.	Interviews
When we have access to information from previous projects.	Lessons learned
When we do not have sufficient in-house knowledge, and have time and budget.	Independent assessments
When we have knowledge to provide a starting point of key areas to consider.	Checklists and templates
When we want to reach consensus on areas of highest risk.	Risk workshops
When we want to gain an initial idea of potential risks.	Brainstorm

ANSWERS TO EXERCISES

Exercise 1 (on page 70)

The best answer is C. Here is the reasoning.

Answer A refers to a time pressure issue, which is a project risk.

Answer B refers to the order of bug fixing, which affects the priority of fixing and testing. This is not a product risk at this time (it may lead to a poorly performing product if the high priority bugs are not identified, but this is not stated).

Answer D refers to a timing issue, which is a project risk.

Exercise 2 (on page 70)

The best answer is B. Here is the reasoning.

Option i is an economic risk since it refers to revenues into the company.

Option ii is a cost associated with the development, and thus is a project risk.

Option iii is about timing of release, so is a project risk.

Option iv is associated with the product itself, so it is a product risk (associated with the hardware this time).

Thus, the correct options are ii and iii.

Exercise 3 (on page 78)

The table shows the outcome of our risk analysis exercise.

Risk ID	Description	Probability	Impact	Score	Mitigation order
A	Poor load handling	L	H	M	2
B	Poor data integrity	M	H	H	1
C	Poor usability	L	L	L	3
D	Poor security	L	H	M	2

Notice here that we allocate the higher risk score for risk B – it has a medium probability, but high impact – playing safe and erring on the side of caution by allocating a higher score will ensure that it is given due consideration in the mitigation plan.

Thus, in our plan, our order of mitigation would be B-D-A-C. We would address the risk of poor data integrity first (risk B), followed by security and load handling (risks D and A), finishing with usability (risk C).

Of course, in the real world, we will have many more risks to deal with and, as you might expect, would be addressing many of them concurrently.

ANSWERS TO EXAMPLE EXAMINATION QUESTIONS

E1 (on page 81)

The correct answer is C. Here is the reasoning.

Option i refers to the functionality of the application. It is not life cycle dependent.

Option ii also refers to application functionality, thus is not dependent on the life cycle being used.

Option iii refers specifically to the V model requirement for high- and low-level designs, and thus is applicable.

Option iv refers to rejection at the final stages of validation, a key risk of the V model.

Thus options iii and iv are the best options.

E2 (on page 81)

The correct answer is A. Here is the reasoning.

The development approach in answer A is the use of object-oriented methods.

Answer B refers to a project risk, it is not specific to the use of object-oriented methods.

Answer C refers to application functionality and its complexity. This is not specific to the use of object-oriented methods.

Answer D is a risk associated with the use of the development life cycle, the V model, not the development approach.

E3 (on page 82)

The correct answer is D. Here is the reasoning.

Answer A refers to usability of the airbags in the car. The upgrade is concerned with airbag deployment, not its impact in use (although this should of course have already been considered before the upgrade was requested).

Answer B refers to an activity independent of the challenges of development. It refers to the finished product, not specifically the ACS upgrade.

Answer C refers to a project risk of a requirement for use of a tool, which may increase costs and introduce a need for training.

4 Test management

BACKGROUND

Test management is a very broad topic and is developed further in the ISEB Test Management Practitioner Certificate syllabus. The coverage of test management at Intermediate level is designed to meet the needs of three groups: those who will go on to a Practitioner level qualification in test management; those who will study test analysis at Practitioner level and who therefore need a rounded introduction to test management; and those who will study up to Intermediate level but do not plan to progress to Practitioner.

In this chapter we cover all the syllabus topics at a level that will ensure you are well prepared for the Intermediate exam, but we will also try to give you a flavour of what practical test management is about.

INTRODUCTION TO TEST MANAGEMENT

Learning objectives

The learning objectives for this chapter are listed below. You can confirm that you have achieved these by using the self-assessment questions on page 88, the 'Check of understanding' boxes distributed through the text, and the example examination questions at the end of the chapter. The chapter summary will remind you of the key ideas.

We have given a K number to each topic to represent the level of understanding required for that topic; for an explanation of the K numbers see Chapter 6 and Appendix B.

Review of Foundation Certificate content

- Review the main principles and themes from relevant areas of the Foundation syllabus, all of which are considered part of the required knowledge for this syllabus. (K1).

Test policy, test strategy, test plans

- Explain the hierarchy of test management and its associated documentation. (K2)
- Describe the role and purpose of each document in the test management hierarchy. (K2)
- Analyse a suite of documentation to determine its effectiveness in defining policy, strategy and plans. (K4)

Test entry and exit criteria
- Explain the significance of objective test entry and exit criteria. (K2)
- Give examples of suitable test entry and exit criteria and explain possible alternative courses of action when test entry and exit criteria are not met. (K2)
- Analyse testing situations to select appropriate test entry and exit criteria. (K4)

Estimating techniques
- Explain the nature and importance of estimation applied to testing. (K2)
- Explain the methods and inputs or parameters available to estimate the time and effort required to design, document, schedule and execute a test or a collection of tests. (K2)
- List different estimation methods, and the value of using more than one method. (K2)
- Explain the difference between an estimate and a target. (K2)
- Explain why more than one cycle or iteration of test execution should be estimated. (K2)
- Analyse a situation to determine the best estimating approach and make estimates of test effort and duration. (K4)

Test monitoring
- Describe how testing may be monitored, and give examples of what could be monitored. (K1)
- Identify and describe typical measures of test progress and test quality. (K2)
- Identify the content of test summary reports appropriate to a range of stakeholders and at different stages of the test process and at different points in the life cycle. (K2)
- Analyse a test summary report to assess the testing reported on and decide on required control actions. (K4)

Incident management process
- Describe how incidents are reported, tracked and analysed to ensure that remedial action is effective. (K2)
- Describe alternative incident management processes. (K2)
- Analyse a simple incident management process and determine what improvements could be made. (K4)

Self-assessment questions

The following questions have been designed to enable you to check your current level of understanding of the topics in this chapter. The answers are provided on page 114.

Question SA1

Which of the following are included in test plans?

i. A schedule of events.

ii. The set of test cases to be run.

iii. The roles and responsibilities of stakeholders.

iv. The test data.

v. The test results and incidents raised.

A. i and ii

B. ii and iii

C. ii, iv and v

D. i and iii

Question SA2

Which of the following would be an appropriate entry criterion from system testing into acceptance testing?

A. 100 per cent functional specification coverage.

B. 100 per cent business requirements coverage.

C. 100 per cent statement coverage.

D. 100 per cent path coverage.

Question SA3

Which of the following would give the best measure of progress against product quality?

A. The number of tests run against those planned.

B. The turnaround time for defects.

C. The number of high priority defects outstanding.

D. The time taken to run each test.

TEST POLICY, TEST STRATEGY, TEST PLANS

The test management document hierarchy

Testing can be managed at different levels.

We can have a very high level of management at an organisational or corporate level. This might be limited to a definition of how testing is expected to be conducted throughout an organisation (e.g. it should always be risk-based).

We can manage testing at programme level. Here, we would detail how testing would be conducted across a series of projects, usually linked in some way (e.g. a bank may have programmes relating to retail banking and investment banking, each managed in different ways). Test management at programme level would be expected to follow any guidance provided at organisational or corporate level.

We can manage testing at individual project level. Here, we would detail the testing necessary to deal with issues specific to an individual project (e.g. within retail banking we may have a project to implement new legislative requirements).

For each of these levels of test management there is an associated document. When structured in a top-down fashion, it is called the test management documentation hierarchy.

An example of this is shown in Figure 4.1. It provides a basic model for test management from which to gain an understanding of the relationships between documents used to manage testing at different levels.

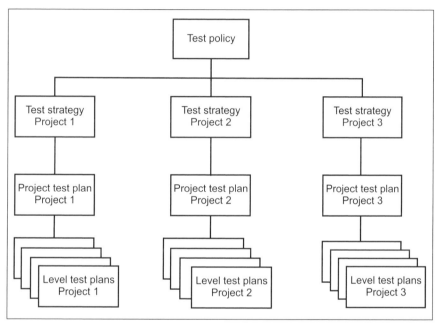

FIGURE 4.1   *Test management documentation hierarchy*

Figure 4.1 might be appropriate to a large organisation with a mature testing culture. The hierarchy identifies a single overall organisational test policy, a test strategy for each individual project, a project test plan for each project and a set of level test plans that elaborate the detailed test planning for each test level of each project. This is a simple and consistent model and so is easy to remember. In practice, the test management documentation encountered in real organisations will vary. The basic hierarchical model in Figure 4.1 provides a way of recognising variations and, more importantly, of understanding whether the variations meet the needs of the organisation.

The Intermediate syllabus is based on such a hierarchical model. In this chapter we will explore some possible variations after we have identified the purpose of each level in the hierarchy.

Test policy

A test policy represents an organisation's overall attitude and approach to testing.

Documented test policies are not all that common, but many organisations have a quality policy which encompasses a definition of what testing must achieve, while others may incorporate quality and testing into a corporate mission statement, such as 'All systems available 24/7'.

There are advantages, however, in having a well-documented test policy. These include:

- visible commitment to the test effort at an organisational level;
- definition of key processes that must be followed;
- definition of quality levels that must be achieved throughout testing.

Typical headings in a test policy are shown in the following box.

TEST POLICY TOPICS

Note that there are no industry-standard headings for a test policy but the following should be considered for inclusion.

- Definition of what 'testing' means in the organisation (i.e. how much testing the organisation expects to be done on software products).
- The test process to be followed (e.g. the Fundamental Test Process).
- General standards and criteria for testing in projects (which may depend on classification of projects as critical, large, small etc.), especially acceptance criteria.
- Use of tools to support testing, including the tool set to be used where appropriate.
- Definition of testing terms such as test level, test type, test condition to clarify their use in other documents.
- How the value of testing will be measured (e.g. by assessing the cost of testing to prevent defects versus the cost of repair when a defect is found).
- Identification of standard software development life cycle(s) and associated testing life cycle(s) used in the organisation.
- The approach to test process improvement (e.g. seeking customer feedback as part of an overall quality plan, staff training).

Thus the test policy defines both what the organisation expects from testing and how it will support the test effort.

An important characteristic of policy is that it is generic. It is intended to apply to every project and provide a framework from which specific test strategies can be developed for individual projects.

Another is that it may also represent a mechanism for encouraging standardisation across projects. Standardisation should in theory yield gains in efficiency and cost reductions. For example, where an organisation has chosen to make a major investment in software testing tools it may mandate the use of tools from a particular tool vendor with whom it has negotiated a favourable set of commercial terms.

Test strategy

The purpose of a test strategy is generally regarded as being to define the overall approach to testing for a specific project or product. In doing this, it must take into account the requirements laid down in a test policy, should one exist.

A test strategy can relate to an organisation, to departments within an organisation or to individual projects. There can be standard test strategy templates, used at a high level across all projects within an organisation, or lower down, across projects of similar functionality (e.g. a bank may have a test strategy template for use by all projects involved in online banking).

At Intermediate level, the syllabus, this book, and the examination will focus on test strategies created to address risks identified for a specific project and associated product. That is, the test strategy will show what is required to deal with specific product risks (such as a feature not working as expected) and specific project risks (such as a vendor not delivering a software package on time).

Documented test strategies are much more common than documented test policies. The term risk-based testing is being used more and more by organisations. The reasons for this include recognition that simply trying to test everything is not likely to be cost-effective (you may recall one of the principles of testing being that 'exhaustive testing is impossible (practically)', as well as recognition that all stakeholders must be included in the quality effort. Stakeholders should be consulted on what is important to them, and what the likely impact of poor functionality or late delivery would be on them.

The benefits of creating a documented test strategy include:

- the business will understand what is required from them in order to conduct testing (such as their assessment of risks, well-defined requirements);
- the project management team will have early detailed knowledge of what will be required for testing and can plan budgets accordingly (such as test tools and the test environment);
- the development team will understand their contribution to the test effort (such as frozen code, 100 per cent decision coverage achieved at unit or integration testing);
- the test team will understand what needs to be done, such as usage of test design technique and criteria they must meet for each stage of testing (usually system and acceptance testing).

TEST STRATEGY TOPICS

Note that, as for the test policy, no definitive industry standard exists for the test strategy, but the following should be considered.

- Standards to be followed (e.g. those required for the defence, transport, pharmaceutical and banking industries to name a few, plus process standards such as the Capability Maturity Model (CMMI) and the International Organization for Standardization quality set – the ISO 9000 set).
- Test levels to be used (such as increased emphasis on user acceptance testing in an iterative model, all levels in the V model).
- Test types to be used (such as functional, structure-based, non-functional testing and experience-based, which you may recall from your ISEB Foundation course).
- Test design techniques to be used (such as equivalence partitioning, decision testing and error guessing).
- Approach to retesting and regression testing (usually all changes will be retested, and regression cycles specified (e.g. weekly or by number of changes included)).
- The amount of testing to be carried out on reused components (depending on the extent of reuse).
- Entry and exit criteria to be used for each level of testing (such as 100 per cent decision coverage at unit and integration test levels).
- Incident management (reporting, follow-up and analysis).
- Definition of test environments to be used.
- Use of tools to support testing.

The list is not exhaustive but provides an indication of what should be covered.

Test plans

Project test plans

The purpose of a test plan is to set out the tasks and resources required to carry out the testing activities defined for a project, within a specific time period. The activities required may have been defined in a test strategy. In this case, the test plan should show how the test strategy will be implemented.

Test planning can take place at two levels: at a high level (called a project test plan) and at a low level (called a phase or level test plan).

A project test plan will show tasks and responsibilities across all test levels, while the level test plan will drill into the detail for each test level (such as named individuals, specific tasks and milestones to be achieved).

From your ISEB Foundation course you may be familiar with the IEEE 829-1998 Standard for Software test documentation. This describes the topics to be considered as part of test planning. (Note that here, test planning encompasses both the requirements for creating a test strategy and a plan.)

In the documentation hierarchy, the test strategy precedes the test plan. The test plan in turn, should include all elements of the test strategy, with the addition of:

- how it will be done – specific tasks to be carried out (e.g. if the strategy requires that performance testing is to be carried out, then the test plan would identify specific tasks, such as identifying performance requirements, acquiring a tool, generating transactions etc.);
- when it needs to be done by – specific deadlines and milestones to be reached;
- who will do it – staffing and training required to carry out the project.

The following box lists the topics required within the IEEE 829-1998 standard. It has been included in this section because it is an industry-recognised standard on software test documentation. It is most well known for its coverage of test planning, but in fact covers other aspects of test documentation, such as test specification and test reporting.

In the ISEB Intermediate examination, you will be expected to recognise that the test plan covers all that was detailed in a test strategy, with the addition of the how, when and who described above.

IEEE 829–1998 TEST PLAN TOPICS

- Test plan identifier
- Introduction
- Test items
- Features to be tested
- Features not to be tested
- Item pass or fail criteria
- Test deliverables
- Responsibilities
- Staffing and training
- Approvals
- Approach
- Testing tasks
- Environmental needs
- Risks and contingencies
- Suspension and resumption criteria
- Schedule

Level test plans

Level test plans achieve for a test level what the project test plan achieves for the project as a whole. Indeed, level test plans may well be sections of the project test plan document, or the project test plan may consist of just a set of references to level test plans with any overarching details documented separately.

EXERCISE 1 – TEST POLICY, TEST STRATEGY, TEST PLANS

1. In which order should the following test management documentation be created?
   - i. Project test plan
   - ii. Test strategy
   - iii. Test policy
   - iv. Level test plan

   A. i, ii, iii, iv
   B. ii, i, iii, iv
   C. iii, ii, i, iv
   D. i, iv, iii, ii

2. Which of the following is a test policy statement?

   A. ToolX within the Efficient tool set will be required for this project.
   B. Projects across the company will make use of the Efficient toolset.
   C. Training will be required in ToolX for staff on this project.
   D. ToolX will be required for a period of one month.

CHECK OF UNDERSTANDING CU1 – WHY POLICY, STRATEGY AND PLANS?

1. What is the purpose of a test policy?
2. What is the purpose of a test strategy?

CHECK OF UNDERSTANDING CU2 – A TEST MANAGEMENT SCENARIO

ABC Ltd has a quality management system (QMS) with a quality policy that includes testing. The documented development and testing life cycle is the V model. All test levels and testing techniques are mandated in the QMS procedures.

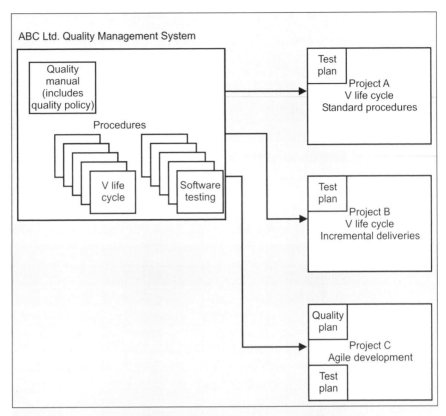

FIGURE 4.2   *ABC Ltd quality management system*

1.   Is this a properly documented test management hierarchy?
2.   How will the test plan for projects A and B differ?
3.   What will the quality plan for project C need to cover?

ENTRY AND EXIT CRITERIA

In testing terms, entry and exit criteria represent the objective criteria that must be met before a test level is entered or exited. Entry and exit criteria can be applied to every test level. The exit criteria from the final test level (typically user acceptance testing) may be known as acceptance criteria or completion criteria, but the difference is in name only and the criteria serve the same purpose as any other exit criteria.

The importance of objective criteria

What do we mean by 'objective criteria'? Objective criteria are not subject to opinion or judgement; they are defined in a way that is either directly measurable or otherwise testable so that there is no doubt or uncertainty associated with whether the criterion is achieved.

For example, if all components must have zero known defects before integration testing can start then zero known component defects is an entry criterion for integration testing. The criterion is an objective one provided defects are formally reported and cleared so that we have an unambiguous way to determine whether the criterion has been met. It might be more realistic to expect zero critical defects rather than zero defects; this is still objective as long as 'critical' is defined and is part of the reporting mechanism for defects.

Why is objectivity so important? Objectivity is important because objective criteria are not open to opinion or manipulation; they are either met or not met and, if they are based on some numerical measure, we can tell how far from meeting the criterion we are. Thus a system with 50 components, of which two have a single critical defect outstanding each, appears to be close to meeting the criteria. We can only tell how close when we have examined the outstanding defects and determined how much time and effort it will take to correct them. Contrast this with a system that has 50 components and 30 of them each have more than one critical defect.

In the first case identified the idea of accepting the risk and proceeding to integration seems reasonable and could be justified as long as the risk associated could be shown to be small and the outstanding defect corrections had been scheduled into a revised plan. In the second case, the risk could be addressed by reprioritising appropriate test activities, after determining how long it will take to correct and retest all the outstanding defects.

If we set objective criteria for every level of testing and we do this at the beginning of the project, then we have a reliable means of determining how close we are to meeting our quality objectives, how much work will be entailed in reaching the objectives from where we are, and how much risk there would be in proceeding without meeting all of the criteria. In other words, we have a way to take the guesswork and emotion out of decision making. This still does not guarantee that we will always make the right decisions but it will make it easier to understand the implications of decisions.

Managing by criteria

There are two important advantages to managing testing projects by making use of objective entry and exit criteria.

- The criteria for successful completion are set at the beginning of the project, well before the pressures associated with delivery are felt, and can be based on a consensus of all the stakeholders.
- Decisions are visible and simple at the transitions from one test level to another and at delivery.

These advantages do not, in themselves, provide any guarantee of a successful project. What they do achieve, however, is to make the decision-making process more open throughout the project. Every stakeholder can see how well the project is progressing against its quality criteria and if any decisions are required to authorise progress beyond a milestone for which the criteria have not been met the implications are clear to all.

At the point of delivery a final release decision will be based on criteria that are met, nearly met or not met. Where the criteria are met the release is straightforward. Where the criteria are nearly met a risk-based decision can be made based on the gap between the criteria and the actual achievement. Where criteria are not met the decision may be more tricky, but even here the existence of objective criteria can help to quantify the level of risk and select the best action plan.

EXERCISE 2 – ENTRY AND EXIT CRITERIA

A development house (DH) uses the V model for its projects. It delivers systems to the energy industry. In response to consumer demands, DH has been asked to create an online system for consumers to switch energy suppliers easily.

There are already offerings in the marketplace for this service, but DH thinks it can provide a service which is easier to use. It will request more detailed information on homes and occupant lifestyles in order to accurately predict likely bills per quarter, and will update users if a cheaper tariff becomes available.

For this new service, the specifications have been defined, code has been created, and system testing is about to start.

1. Which of the following could form part of the entry criteria into system testing?

    i. 100 per cent decision coverage of all tariff calculations.

    ii. 100 per cent functional specification coverage of all household types.

    iii. Outstanding defects at integration testing highlighted.

    iv. Test summary report for system testing produced.

    v. Business requirements signed off.

    A. i, ii and iii
    B. ii, iii and iv
    C. i and iii
    D. i, iii and iv

2. Which of the following would form part of the entry criteria into unit testing (which will be followed by integration testing)?

    i. 100 per cent decision coverage of all tariff calculations.

    ii. Signed-off program specification.

    iii. Signed-off technical specification.

    iv. 100 per cent program specification coverage.

    v. Compiled code.

A. i, iii and v
B. ii and v
C. i, ii and iii
D. iii, iv and v

WORKED EXAMPLE – RELEASE DECISIONS

A system has the following among its acceptance criteria:

- Zero critical (level 1) defects outstanding.
- Not more than five level 2 defects outstanding.
- Not more than 10 total defects outstanding.
- All (prioritised) requirements tested.
- 100 per cent statement and decision coverage.

At the planned release date the system has achieved 75 per cent of requirements tested, with one critical defect, two level 2 defects, and a total of 15 defects at any level outstanding. Code coverage of the code tested is 100 per cent statement coverage and 80 per cent decision coverage.

Clearly the system has not met the acceptance criteria. Just over three quarters of the prioritised requirements have been tested, so most high risk or high value areas of the system have been tested. Code coverage is incomplete but still fairly high. The critical defect is, by definition, too serious to allow immediate release.

What options do we have? Release could only be authorised if the nature of the critical defect was known and an adequate work around could be found. An estimate of the time to correct and retest this defect is needed urgently. Based on that estimate a short delay could be authorised, during which the critical defect would be corrected and tested; other routine testing could continue and other defects could be corrected (as long as enough resource is available). If this delay was short a decision to release could be given subject to successful testing of the fixed critical defect, knowing that performance against the other criteria will be improved by the new release date (unless new critical defects emerge). This seems a sensible approach.

As an alternative, a decision could be made to defer release until the criteria are met in full.

In a real situation the time and other pressures will determine which option is best. Knowledge of the gaps enables a reasonably accurate estimate to be made of the risk of any decision, and it also provides a basis for any actions necessary to reduce the risk of a release when all criteria are not met, such as making an extended support facility available with staff specifically trained to deal with problems related to areas of the system known to have weaknesses.

ESTIMATING TECHNIQUES

Estimates and targets

An estimate is a guess or a judgement based on what is known about a situation.

For example, we can estimate the completion date of a project based on the nature and size of the project and the resources available.

A deadline is a date for delivery, which, if not met, may hamper business activities.

If the estimate for completion and the deadline are significantly different something must be done to reconcile the difference. If the deadline is paramount then the parameters from which the estimates were made will need to be changed to enable a different conclusion to be reached, usually by accepting greater risk or reducing the expected quality of the project deliverables. If the estimate is taken as the measure of what can be achieved then the deadline must be rethought. In practice, both actions may be taken to reach a compromise solution.

In practice, estimating is seldom very accurate, which can make compromise difficult to reach. This may result in projects that are driven by unachievable deadlines, leading to either late delivery or poor quality of delivery. Achievement of an accurate and well-documented estimate of time and effort is therefore of vital significance to test managers.

Estimation parameters

Anything can be estimated, but the usual need in a project is an estimate of the effort and time needed to complete the testing.

The effort required in software testing will depend on a number of factors. These include:

- the size of the development effort (perhaps measured in time taken, number of lines of code or overall complexity of the code that will be delivered into test);
- the amount code which is being reused from previous projects. This may require less testing (bearing in mind the issues of compatibility of reused components with functionality in the new system);
- the rigour of exit criteria which have been set – 100 per cent code or requirements coverage would suggest extensive testing required at developer and tester levels;
- use of automated tools. These could reduce timescales if already in use, or extend them if being used in earnest for the first time;
- levels of experience of the testers – the more experienced, the less time (in theory) required;
- the test environment – its stability will affect test execution timescales.

In making an estimate of testing effort we need to take account of the whole test process, from analysis through to execution and test closure. This entails estimating the time and effort required to design and script tests as well as executing them. Testing will lead to incidents, so we will need to estimate the time it will take to document incidents and subsequently complete retesting and regression testing. Much will depend on the expectation of quality because this will affect the number of incidents raised and the volume of retesting and regression testing.

It would be impossible to estimate from first principles with this level of detail for every project, which is one reason for the emergence of the estimating methods that we will consider next, but the underlying processes on which estimates are based should always be kept in mind so that any significant process variations can be taken into account.

Estimating methods

There are six main techniques for estimation, ranging from guesswork to using industry-recognised formulae.

- **Intuition-based** – This, as its name suggests, is based on the experience of the person who will carry out the testing. The figure can vary in accuracy, but if it is being done by the person who will carry out the testing, then it can prove to be very accurate in practice.

- **Group consensus** – This is a slightly safer option than the intuition of an individual, if enough people with the right knowledge and experience can be found to contribute. The main characteristic of consensus decisions is that they tend to avoid extremes, so this can be used as a smoothing option.

- **Metrics-based** – This estimation method uses data collected from previous projects as the basis of new estimates. The accuracy of this relies on the availability of accurate metrics, but it also needs the metrics to be related to projects that have enough similarity with the project in hand to be relevant.

- **Detailed work breakdown structure** – An example of a simple work breakdown structure based on the Fundamental Test Process is shown in Figure 4.3. The idea underlying this approach is that most people can estimate a small and simple task more easily than a large and complex one, so if we can break all the tasks down to their simplest level and estimate them individually, we can then build up an overall estimate. This is known as a bottom-up estimate (i.e. we start with the individual tasks and work up to an overall figure for an activity). Clearly a detailed work breakdown structure requires a detailed understanding of the task, and this almost certainly means a detailed specification of some kind. It is also the case that an estimator with limited experience may not be able to accurately estimate all the different tasks in the work breakdown structure. For a reasonably experienced estimator this is a sound approach. There is a disadvantage, however, in that inaccuracies at each task level will add up to an overall less accurate figure.

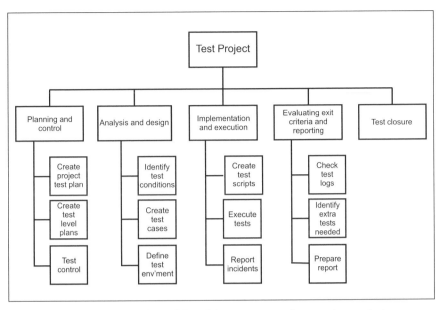

FIGURE 4.3   *Basic work breakdown structure for a testing project*

- **Percentage of development effort** – This is a top-down approach to estimation. The whole of the development effort is considered and a portion of this allocated to testing. The percentage applied can be based on in-house experience or industry figures (these give a figure of between 35–50 per cent). This estimate is very coarse, providing only an approximation of the total testing effort for the project with no detail of how this is likely to be broken down by test levels or test activities. It is used when little detail about the project is known, but there is some knowledge of likely development effort.

- **Test point analysis (TPA)** – This is a formula-based approach, but unlike percentage of development effort, is bottom-up and based on detailed specifications, knowledge of testing tasks and experience of testers. TPA starts with function point analysis (FPA). In FPA, a specification is broken down into its specific function points (such as internal calculations, external data inputs/outputs etc.). For each function point, a set of test points is derived. Each test point is then estimated, based on its complexity and tester experience, among other things.

You can immediately see that estimation needs data and specifications, so one worthwhile action for any organisation is to initiate the collection of test project data as a first step in improving estimation capability.

In addition, it is advisable to use more than one estimating method to arrive at an estimate and then compare the outcomes. The investigation of significant differences can provide a mechanism for exploring the assumptions and parameters underlying each of the estimates, enabling a better single estimate to be derived.

Estimating a test project

It will be clear by now that estimating a complete test project is a challenging undertaking, requiring experience, intuition and skills in using defined techniques.

It is worth remembering that the provision of an estimate does not suggest a prediction of exactly what will happen, but a best guess based on what is known at the time the estimate is made. More information will generally lead to better estimates, and feedback from actual activities will help to improve on the accuracy of future estimates. As a result, estimates will improve as the project progresses.

EXERCISE 3 – ESTIMATION

A local council employs its own IT staff; there are 40, most of whom have been with the council for over 10 years.

The council uses the Agile development methodology. Each project has between five and nine team members, all of whom work very closely together.

At the start of each iteration, the requirements are loosely defined. These are then built, tested and refined.

The IT Department has been asked to upgrade the council website to include:

- information on recycling targets;
- amounts recycled per month; and
- energy usage in the recycling effort.

The project will be undertaken in three iterations, one for each requirement defined above.

Which two of the following methods of test estimation would be most appropriate in this situation?

i.   Making use of a work breakdown structure.

ii. Taking 30 per cent of the total iteration time.

iii. Calculating the time required using test point analysis.

iv. Gaining consensus from the team.

A. i and ii

B. ii and iii

C. i and iv

D. ii and iv

TEST MONITORING

The purpose of the test monitoring activity is to gain an understanding of project progress, as early as possible, so that controlling actions can be taken when they will be most effective.

Monitoring the testing project

Testing projects usually have two main sets of objectives to achieve.

- Those relating to time and cost – will the project be delivered on time and to budget?
- Those relating to quality – will the delivered product be acceptable to its user base?

Monitoring against time and cost

In monitoring how long we are taking and how much it is costing, we can compare the time taken against the estimates for the test activities. These include the following:

- Preparation of test strategies and plans.
- Design of test cases and preparation of test scripts.
- Set-up of the test environment.
- Test execution.
- Number of defects being found, which when addressed, would require rerunning of tests.
- Preparation of test summary reports.

This is important data but potentially even more valuable are the metrics that can be generated from the data, such as:

- number of tests run to number of tests planned;
- test pass rate;
- incidents raised per test;
- rate of incident clearance.

The metrics provide valuable trend information, especially if presented in graphical form; they enable some prediction of what is likely to happen in the future and whether the planned completion date is still feasible and practicable.

Monitoring against quality

In monitoring against quality, we move our focus away from the steps in the test process to the amount of testing actually achieved. These are usually measured against:

- The percentage of statements, decisions, paths etc. tested (i.e. the code coverage achieved). This is usually measured at unit and integration testing.
- The percentage of business critical features tested or requirements coverage achieved. This is usually measured at system and acceptance test levels.
- Rate at which defects are being found and fixed (by severity and priority).

In monitoring against quality, trends are even more valuable for prediction of quality at completion, with metrics such as:

- code coverage achieved to code coverage planned (for every code coverage measure used in exit criteria);
- percentage of requirements tested to date;
- rate of occurrence of critical defects;
- rate of clearance of critical defects;
- projected time to achieve completion criteria.

Trends are essential in determining whether and when a project will reach its planned completion criteria. If the prediction of completion slips back then some action must be considered to manage the situation.

Determining the overall status of the project

The overall status of the project can be determined by monitoring progress against time, cost and quality. Progress and quality measures provide an accurate picture of where the project is and the associated metrics provide the trend information that enables some prediction of completion to be attempted.

Of course the measurements and trends may not provide a straightforward picture. If all measures show that the project is on track and trends suggest on-time completion then all appears well. If test progress and test quality data both show significant slippage and trend information shows that the slippage is increasing we have an equally clear though less palatable picture.

The more common and more interesting scenarios, though, arise when the data and trends give us a mixed picture. For example, the test progress data and trends may indicate that testing activity is running to plan and will complete on time, while the test quality data and trends indicate slippage against the expected date for achieving the completion criteria. In this case it would appear that the project may not meet its quality objectives by the planned release date. This will require careful consideration. It could be that the project is generating more defects than expected because the quality of deliverables is lower than had been anticipated; it could be that the test plan was optimistic about how much testing would need to be done to identify defects and then subsequently retest and regression test after defect correction. This situation is one in which the detailed trend information for the whole project will be invaluable in determining what is actually happening.

What about the case where quality progress is running ahead of schedule because fewer defects are being found than had been anticipated, and test progress is on schedule? While that looks like a positive picture, can we be sure that the testing is actually identifying all the defects? It may be that the testing is insufficiently rigorous and that this will become evident later in the project. This situation needs to be examined just as carefully as the more negative one, and again the trend information is the key to analysing what is happening.

Measurement for process improvement

If measures and metrics are being collected and analysed, it would make sense to include some that will provide a basis for determining how well testing is progressing over the longer term. Are we getting better at identifying defects early? Are we reaching our exit criteria consistently on time?

What measures are needed for this kind of monitoring? Time and analysis will help to refine measures collected for process improvement, but we could at least have a simple 'shopping list' of measures and metrics to provide a starting point, especially if they can be collected at the same time as the essential progress and quality measures and at little or no extra cost.

If we look ahead to how the measures and metrics will be used, a key component will be some characterisation of the project, so that we know which projects are comparable. The nature of the project in terms of number of requirements and volume of code, the complexity of the project in terms such as number of business rules implemented, the size of the development and test teams, the elapsed time planned and achieved, will be important in future comparisons. The test techniques and tools used will be worth recording (a copy of the test strategy could be saved for this purpose). The development and test life cycle and development methods used will be of interest. Armed with this background we can then look at standardised metrics such as defects discovered per line of code, defects per day of testing, defects per phase, length in days of each phase, number of tests planned and so on. The initial list will be your best guess about what questions you think you will want to ask in the future, but this will inevitably be refined over time.

Selecting control actions

One purpose of test monitoring is to enable effective and timely action. The choice of control actions for the test manager may be limited, but a well-constructed report based on sound data and trend information will be essential in gaining support from other stakeholders for action. The test manager may be able to modify testing priorities or even possibly add testing resources to make up a shortfall, but more far-reaching action, such as modifying the scope of a software release or deferring the release date, will need the project manager and probably other stakeholders to agree. It is extremely unlikely that anything less than a well-argued case based on detailed data analysis will enlist support in such a case.

EXERCISE 4 – TEST MONITORING/TEST CONTROL

In monitoring progress against the test plan for the scenario in Exercise 3 on page 102, which of the following measures would be required at the end of iteration 2?

i.   Number of defects found and fixed in 'recycling targets' and 'energy usage' calculations.

ii. Percentage of tests run for 'amounts recycled'.

iii. Number of high priority defects outstanding in 'amounts recycled'.

iv. Defect turnaround time for 'energy usage'.

A. i and ii

B. ii and iii

C. iii and iv

D. i and iv

Test summary reporting

Test summary reporting might be better termed test status reporting. What stakeholders need to know is 'where are we and when will we be ready to release the software?' All the measures and metrics should be used to create a clear picture that answers those two questions. The first thing they will want to know is the status of any outstanding risks, especially any that have arisen since the last report. Test progress and test quality measures can then tell us where we are, and metrics enable us to predict when we will be ready to release. Beyond this each stakeholder needs to know what action is being taken to resolve any problems, and what they can specifically do to improve the likelihood of a successful outcome.

Test summary reporting will need to be presented in a way that is appropriate for each stakeholder. The test manager, for example, will need to know all of the detailed measures and metrics with as much graphical support as possible and a thorough analysis of the trends and possible alternative outcomes with recommendations for action.

We might consider this the 'Master Test Summary Report' because all other reports can be generated by summarising and manipulating the contents of this version of the report content. The master report will, in all probability, be culled from a number of sources, with each test team leader providing a simpler report for their own team's activities. The detailed content of a test summary report will vary according to the nature of the life cycle in use, the associated testing methods and the stage in the life cycle at which the report is produced, but a template can be used to provide a framework that can be adapted in each case. For example, in an iterative development a test summary report might be produced for each timebox. In this situation defect trends will be less meaningful since the requirements baseline is moving, but the number of requirements implemented and tested in the timebox to date, the number of requirements untested in the timebox and the regression testing details from the timebox will give the test manager good visibility of progress.

At this point it would be appropriate to raise the question of who gathers the data and calculates the trends, and how the collection and calculation tasks are distributed around the project. This is a more advanced topic that will be considered at the Test Manager Practitioner level, but it is important to consider it in a practical context, because reporting will only be effective if data collection and trend information are thorough and accurate, and this means allocating resources to the task.

It would not be feasible to specify exactly what each stakeholder's test summary report might look like, but here is a flavour of two of the variations we might expect to see.

TEST SUMMARY REPORT OUTLINES

The project manager will want to know the impact of testing on the project as a whole. This is likely to include:

- a high-level summary, with a graph, of test progress and test quality trends;
- an indication of whether the trends threaten the project's overall timescale and cost;
- notes on any actions in hand to ameliorate potential problems;
- notes on any new risks with proposed risk mitigation actions;
- notes on any issue needing the project manager's attention.

The development manager would need a similar but simpler summary along the following lines:

- a high-level summary, with a graph, of test progress and test quality trends;
- notes on status of defects, especially trends related to defect correction times;
- notes on critical outstanding defects;
- notes on any development issues affecting testing, such as projected late delivery of a work product;
- notes on any specific actions agreed with or required from the development team.

The aim is to provide the level of detail and the kind of analysis needed by the stakeholder. The information must be relevant to the stakeholder's interests and presented in the clearest possible way.

INCIDENT MANAGEMENT

Incident management, the principal mechanism for identifying, recording and resolving issues with the software under test, is a vital part of the software testing discipline. The primary aim is to ensure that no incident remains unresolved, though outcomes from incident analysis may take many forms.

It is important to bear in mind that an incident is so called to differentiate it from a defect. In reporting an incident we identify anything that we believe needs investigation. An incident may report a difference between the expected and actual result of a test, which could be due to a defect in the software under test or in the test itself, or a host of other things, hence the caution about initially declaring an incident as anything more than a situation requiring investigation. Also, in keeping with the principle that defects found early are the easiest and cheapest to correct at the time of discovery, we apply the incident management process as early as possible to ensure that incidents related to requirements (the most common source of defects and the most important to correct) are captured and resolved. In fact, incident management can be and should apply to anything that is recorded in a project, from requirements through development, testing and delivery of software and on to user manuals.

The incident management process

The international standard IEEE 1044 defines a basic process which comprises four steps:

- Recognition
- Investigation
- Action
- Disposition

The standard also identifies three administrative processes associated with each of the steps:

- Recording
- Classifying
- Identifying impact

In this section we will outline how and when these basic steps and processes may be implemented, what their role is, and what their impact is on the overall testing discipline.

Figure 4.4 shows the main steps.

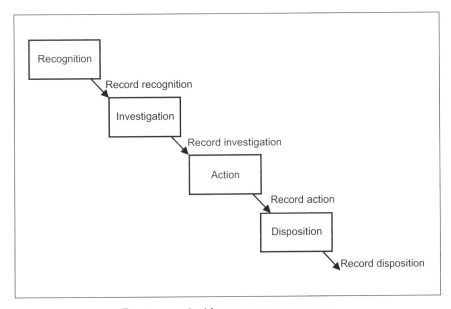

FIGURE 4.4   *Incident management process*

The incident management process may be simple or more complex. A simple process would have the sole aim of identification, tracking and resolution of incidents, while a more complex process might have the additional aims of improving development and testing processes by analysis of incident data. The implementation of an incident management process can also be as simple as a set of linked spreadsheets or as complex as a dedicated tool to record, track and analyse all incident data. One key element of incident management implementations is the management of workflow processes to ensure that every incident is effectively and efficiently tracked through all the phases of the process.

Recognition

The recognition stage is the point at which an incident is first recognised and recorded. The information gathered here is vital because the processes of analysis and ultimate action will depend on it. There are many alternative mechanisms for recognising and recording the necessary details of an incident and these will be explored later. The recognition stage is where the impact of an incident is assessed and priority set for resolution. Details need to be recorded so that investigation can begin.

Information recorded at the recognition stage will depend on the level of investigation desired and the breadth of any actions to resolve the incident. Incident reports vary widely to suit the particular mechanism used in a given organisation, but some information is vital to all incidents. This would include:

- the nature of the incident (e.g. symptoms witnessed);
- when, where and how the incident arose;
- the configuration of the software under test, the test environment and the tests;
- information to enable the incident to be reproduced;
- the seriousness of the incident.

Typically more information than this will be recorded by mechanisms such as selecting options from a classification scheme, entering text into fields on a screen, or writing the information down in longhand.

Investigation

The purpose of the investigation stage is to determine the nature of the incident and any action that needs to be taken to resolve it. The analysis of the incident may be restricted to that required for resolution or it may aim to relate the incident to other similar incidents or past incidents to discern patterns and identify possible process improvements. Details of the investigation and any recommendations for action need to be documented.

Action

The main action stage is to resolve the incident, but action may also be taken to revise processes to avoid recurrence of the same or similar incidents or to avoid potential problems revealed by the investigation. Action taken needs to be documented to enable the incident to be finally resolved.

Disposition

The disposition stage is the final closure of the incident following completion of all appropriate actions. Where the actions include any changes to resolve the incident, successful testing of the changes and any necessary regression testing will be conditions of closure.

Mechanisms and tools

Incident management mechanisms vary widely, but all must have certain core characteristics:

- The ability to record all necessary details of an incident and any subsequent investigation and action.
- The ability to access incident records by some means.

- The ability to determine the status of any incident.
- The communication of incident status and any requirement for action to the appropriate person for the next step.
- A set of rules and responsibilities that define under what circumstances an incident can progress from one step to the next and under whose authority.
- A mechanism for closing the incident record once all actions are cleared (the incident disposal).

The characteristics define a workflow that could be implemented via a sophisticated workflow management software package, by a set of custom built tools with linking process rules, or by humans using pen and paper. The choice of mechanism depends on many factors, including the volume of incidents, the requirements for detailed analysis, the cost of the mechanism and the benefits that are expected to accrue from it.

Incident management has become a fairly standard function of test management tools and some test execution tools, typically providing workflow management, secure storage of incident records and some level of incident analysis. Many organisations, nevertheless, choose to use minimal automation using standard office products such as spreadsheets.

EXERCISE 5 – INCIDENT MANAGEMENT PROCESS ANALYSIS

A simple incident management process has been created. It consists of an incident report template, with the following headings:

- System under test
- Description of incident
- Impact of incident on the system

This report is sent to the developers, who log the problem and issue a request number. All incidents are addressed in strict order of receipt. Once the fix has been made, the person raising the report is notified. The incident is then closed.

Identify improvements to this process.

SUMMARY

In this chapter we have reviewed the Foundation syllabus material on test management and extended it to a fuller treatment, adding new content to provide the fundamental basis for the test management discipline.

The hierarchy of test management documentation was outlined, showing how policy affects test strategies, how test strategies are elaborated in project test plans and how project test plans may be further subdivided into level test plans. The absence of any universally recognised standards for these documents provides for flexibility in implementation and means that no rigid structures can be assumed in any particular organisation.

Test strategies and plans need concrete objectives to ensure projects are properly defined and that successful outcomes can be differentiated from failed projects. One of the most important mechanisms is the use of exit criteria to set specific goals for an activity. Exit criteria can be used to define success at the end of any activity, test level or project, so this concept has multiple uses within software testing projects. Entry criteria can also be used where it is necessary to decide entry to an activity based on factors other than success of a previous activity.

Planning also depends on good estimating of time and resources so we explored estimating methods and the limitations of each of them. Given the difficulty of gathering accurate information on which to base estimates, the value of using multiple methods and the importance of basing estimates on realistic assumptions were both emphasised.

Once a plan has been initiated the next challenge is to ensure its successful completion, which requires careful monitoring of progress so that appropriate action can be taken promptly if actual progress diverges from what is needed for success. Various measures and metrics and their uses in monitoring and control were introduced and explained.

Finally the vital process of incident reporting and management was explored.

The importance of analysis of scenarios was emphasised and examples were given to enable you to practise this key skill.

There is a mind map of the chapter in Appendix A.

EXAMPLE EXAMINATION QUESTIONS

Scenario 1

A major bank has recently outsourced all of its software development in an effort to reduce its fixed costs. The new supplier will be responsible for all new developments as well as enhancements to existing ones.

The bank has retained its own management team for its projects. There will be an in-house project manager, development manager and test manager for each project. Some staff may work on more than one project, depending on the overall size.

An enhancement is being made to allow existing customers to authorise their own loans online, from £1k to £10k by answering a series of questions.

E1

Which of the following best describes the usefulness of a test policy in this scenario?

A. The test policy will ensure that all members from both sets of teams understand what their roles and responsibilities are.
B. The test policy will identify the risks of each project, and ensure that all staff knows how to deal with them.
C. The test policy will ensure that all team members understand what is required by the bank to create high quality products.
D. The test policy will remind staff of the usefulness of using their own knowledge to conduct testing.

E2

You are a test manager with the bank and you have written a test strategy for the outsourced team to follow. Unit testing has begun but informal conversations with the developers have revealed that they have not received a signed-off specification from the bank for the enhancement. They do know how loans work though and have created code from conversations with bank staff alongside their own knowledge.

How could a strategy have helped to avoid this situation?

A. The test strategy would have identified bank staff with the right knowledge for consultation on the loan requirements.
B. The test strategy would have laid out the process for capturing how the loan process would work which the outsourced team would have followed.
C. The test strategy would have specified that a signed-off specification would be made available to the coding team prior to the start of development.
D. The test strategy would have requested that the outsourced team take part in specifying the requirements, to make use of their knowledge.

Scenario 2

The aircrew of a national air defence force has requested changes to the existing aviation software that provides on-board information about the combat environment. The air force is currently engaged in a peace-keeping mission in another country and has come under unexpected threats.

The development life cycle is the V model. The software house needs to change their test management process to ensure delivery at the right time and quality.

The software changes are coming in as the aircrew request them, as a result of their engagements with hostile forces.

The aircrew have requested that the changes are made as quickly as possible. The project manager has decided to revisit the test management process. The changes will come as small change requests. The team have worked on the project for over 25 years, with little staff turnover.

E3

The project manager has asked for your advice on test estimation. Which of the following would you recommend?

A. Conduct a test point analysis on each change request definition.
B. Analyse data from previous projects to find changes similar to each change request, and use this to estimate the time required.
C. Ask the developers how long the change will take to implement and allocate 50 per cent of this to testing.
D. Ask the tester who will be doing the testing for a best guess.

E4

Which of the following test measures should be emphasised during the crisis?

i. Readiness of the test environment for each run.
ii. Number of high-priority defects being found.
iii. Number of defects being found per tester.
iv. Number of hours overtime being worked by staff.
v. Number of change requests tested versus number passed.

A. i, ii and v
B. ii, iii and iv
C. ii, iii and v
D. i, ii and iii

ANSWERS TO SELF-ASSESSMENT QUESTIONS (ON PAGE 88)

SA1. D
SA2. A
SA3. C

ANSWERS TO CHECKS OF UNDERSTANDING

CU1 (on page 94)

1. The purpose of a test policy is to set out a set of rules and guidelines that, ideally, should be followed for all projects.
2. The purpose of a test strategy is to show the activities required in order to mitigate the project and product risks identified for a *particular project*. Note that a test strategy is specific to a project, while the test policy should apply across all projects.

CU2 (on page 94)

1. Provided testing is adequately covered in procedures and test plans have a strategy component this would be a properly documented test management hierarchy.
2. We would expect the test plan for project B to explain how incremental deliveries will differ from standard procedures and define how testing for incremental deliveries will be handled.
3. The quality plan for project C will need to define the differences between Agile development and development done with the V life cycle, effectively defining an Agile testing strategy. The test plan would then define how the strategy would be implemented in the project.

CU3 (on page 102)

Here we have reordered the table to show the best match between the method of estimation and its usage.

Method	Best used when
Based on intuition	We have experience in similar systems.
Based on a group consensus	We have access to people with experience of similar systems.
Metrics-based	We have access to relevant data collected from previous projects.
Based on a work breakdown structure	We understand the activities involved in carrying out a particular testing task.
Based on a percentage of development effort	We have limited relevant experience, but we do know the likely development effort.
Based on test point analysis	We have a fully defined specification and we are not in a hurry.

ANSWERS TO EXERCISES

Exercise 1 (on page 94)

1. The correct answer is C. Here is the reasoning.
   The test policy should be written first, to be applied across the organisation. The strategy should be written next, to deal with the risks identified and prioritised for a particular project. This should be followed by a project test plan, showing how the test strategy will be implemented at a high level, followed by a level test plan, showing the specific tasks, deadlines, roles and responsibilities for each test level.
2. The correct answer is B. Here is the reasoning.

Answer A refers to a specific project, this would be expected in the test strategy.

Answer C refers to training for a specific project, this will appear in a test plan.

Answer D mentions a specific tool for a specified time period. This would be expected in a test plan.

Exercise 2 (on page 97)

1. The correct answer is C. Here is the reasoning.

   Option i, '100 per cent decision coverage of tariff calculations', could form part of the exit criteria from unit and integration testing, which could then become part of the entry criteria for system testing. Therefore, this is a suitable option.

   Option ii, '100 per cent functional specification coverage', would form part of the exit criteria from system testing. Therefore, this is unsuitable.

   Option iii, 'outstanding defects highlighted at integration testing', could form part of the exit criteria from integration testing, and thus form part of the entry criteria into system testing.

   Option iv, 'test summary report produced for system testing', will be done at defined checkpoints and at the end of system testing, not at the beginning. Therefore, this would not be part of the entry criteria into system testing.

   Option v, 'sign-off of the business requirements', would form part of the entry criteria into acceptance testing, not system testing.

   Therefore, only options i and iii are suitable.

2. The correct answer is B. Here is the reasoning.

   Option i, '100 per cent decision coverage', would form part of the exit criteria out of unit testing, not the entry criteria.

   Option ii, 'a signed-off program specification', is valid as an entry criterion into unit testing (although very rare in the real world!).

   Option iii, 'a signed-off technical specification', would apply at integration testing.

   Option iv, '100 per cent coverage of the program specification', would form part of the exit criteria out of unit testing.

   Option v, 'compiled code', should be a given, but is relevant as an entry criterion into unit testing.

   Thus options ii and v are suitable as entry criteria into unit testing.

Exercise 3 (on page 102)

The correct answer is C. Here is the reasoning.

Option i, 'a work-breakdown structure', could be used here because we have experienced staff and requirements definitions (albeit loosely defined at first).

Option ii, 'taking a random percentage of development time', is not ideal because we do have experience. The scenario does not suggest that the iteration time is known upfront, and in iterative development is likely to change.

Option iii, 'using test point analysis', is very time-consuming and requires fully defined specifications. The scenario states that these will evolve.

Option iv, 'gaining consensus', is useful since the team does work closely together.

Thus options i and iv are most useful.

Exercise 4 (on page 106)

The correct answer is B. Here is the reasoning.

Option i, 'number of defects found and fixed', refers to 'energy usage', which is at iteration 3, not iteration 2 as the question asks.

Option ii refers to tests run at iteration 2 for 'amounts recycled' and is therefore valid.

Option iii refers to defects outstanding for iteration 2 and is therefore relevant.

Option iv refers to 'energy usage', which will be relevant at iteration 3, not iteration 2.

Thus options ii and iii are relevant.

Exercise 5 (on page 111)

The incident report requires more headings, such as:

- unique ID
- operating platform
- requirement under test
- test procedure ID
- whether the incident is repeatable
- steps to reproduce
- actual results
- expected results
- priority rating
- severity rating
- response by designer or developer
- closure code.

Incidents need addressing. This sounds like a help desk facility, not a development environment. Priority and severity codes should be established. The developers should fix according to the priority and severity ratings allocated. There should be an agreed turnaround time for different priority fixes. There should be a release note with each fix to say what has changed. The incident should not be closed until a fix has been made and it has been retested or a decision has been taken (in conjunction with all managers) that no action is required.

ANSWERS TO EXAMPLE EXAMINATION QUESTIONS

E1 (on page 112)

The correct answer is C. Here is the reasoning.

Answer A is very specific to this project, it mentions both sets of teams. This is more likely to form part of a test plan.

Answer B describes the purpose of a test strategy (i.e. to deal with risks to a specific project).

Answer D is a rather bland statement and is unlikely to form part of a test policy.

E2 (on page 113)

The correct answer is C. Here is the reasoning.

Option A is about requirements capture, not testing. It may appear in a test plan, which may show how reviews of specifications may be carried out, but would not appear in the test strategy (which would say that reviews will be carried out, but would not name specific individuals).

Answer B is again about requirements capture, it would not appear in the test strategy.

Answer D is also about capturing the requirements.

E3 (on page 114)

The correct answer is D. Here is the reasoning.

Answer A, while possible in a safety critical environment (under the reasonable assumption that the change requests would be fully defined) would be too time-consuming for this situation.

Answer B assumes that data is readily available. If not, then it may take a long time to gather the data required.

Answer C gives an arbitrary figure of 50 per cent of development time.

Answer D, while seemingly trivial for a safety-critical project, offers up the best choice in this scenario given the significant experience of the team.

E4 (on page 114)

The correct answer is A. Here is the reasoning.

Option i, 'readiness of the test environment', while it may be a given, should always be monitored.

Option ii, 'number of high-priority defects found', is a good indicator of product quality and should be included.

Option iii, 'number of defects found per tester', may be useful, but it would need to be combined with other data, such as requirements tested to be of any real value.

Option iv, 'number of overtime hours worked by testers', is unlikely to be of much concern here.

Option v, 'number of change requests passing', should be monitored.

This leads us to answer A.

5 Test analysis and design

BACKGROUND

Test analysis, like test management covered in Chapter 4, is developed more fully at Practitioner level in the Test Analysis Practitioner Certificate syllabus. The coverage of test analysis and design at Intermediate level is designed partly to prepare those who will go on to a Practitioner level qualification in test analysis by providing a basis for study up to the K6 level, and partly for those who will study up to Intermediate level but do not plan to progress to Practitioner. It also gives those who will study test management at Practitioner level a rounded introduction to test analysis at a level above that covered by Foundation.

In this chapter we cover all the syllabus topics at a level that will ensure you are well prepared for the Intermediate examination, but we will also try to give you a well-rounded flavour of what test analysis is really about.

INTRODUCTION TO TEST ANALYSIS AND DESIGN

Learning objectives

The learning objectives for this chapter are listed below. You can confirm that you have achieved these by using the self-assessment questions on page 120, the 'Check of understanding' boxes distributed through the text, and the example examination questions at the end of the chapter. The chapter summary will remind you of the key ideas.

We have given a K number to each topic to represent the level of understanding required for that topic; for an explanation of the K numbers see Chapter 6 and Appendix B.

Review of Foundation Certificate content
- Review the main principles and themes from relevant areas of the Foundation syllabus, all of which are considered part of the required knowledge for this syllabus. (K1)

Fundamentals of test analysis
- Define the test analysis function. (K2)
- Recall the basic relationships between test basis, test condition, test case and test procedure (manual test script). (K1)

Test environment requirements
- Identify and explain the principles behind determination of test environment needs for executing tests. (K2)
- Analyse a situation to determine test environment requirements. (K4)

Selection of techniques

- Recognise alternative approaches to testing, including the fundamental differences between static and dynamic testing and between scripted and unscripted testing, and describe the strengths, weaknesses and appropriate uses of each. (K2)
- Describe the categories of test techniques available to testers. (K2)
- Describe possible criteria for selecting test design techniques. (K2)
- Explain the benefits and pitfalls of deploying test design techniques. (K2)
- Analyse a practical testing situation and select appropriate test design techniques.(K4)

Coverage measures

- Explain the concept of coverage and recognise and define suitable measures of coverage. (K2)
- Explain the importance of defining what coverage measures mean in a practical situation. (K2)
- Analyse a practical testing situation and select appropriate coverage measures. (K4)

Self-assessment questions

The following questions have been designed to enable you to check your current level of understanding for the topics in this chapter. The answers are provided on page 142.

Question SA1

Consider the following statements:

i. Functional specification for Crunch3000 products.
ii. Mortgages will only be offered to those with a deposit of 25 per cent of the property value.
iii. Enter a property value of £100k and a mortgage value of £90k. Display shows 'Mortgage not to be offered'.
iv. Test cases will be executed in the following order: TC1, TC3, TC2, TC4.

Consider the following items:

1. p. Test basis
2. q. Test procedure
3. r. Test case
4. s. Test condition

Which of the following accurately matches the items with the statements?

A. i–p, ii–q, iii–r, iv–s
B. i–p, ii–s, iii–r, iv–q

C. i–q, ii–r, iii–s, iv–p
D. i–r, ii–p, iii–q, iv–s

Question SA2

Consider the following test design techniques:

a.   Equivalence partitioning
b.   State transition testing
c.   Decision testing
d.   Decision table testing
e.   Path testing
f.   Modified condition decision testing.
   Which are specification-based techniques?

A. a, b and d
B. a, c and e
C. b, d and f
D. b, d and e

Question SA3

Which of the following is a measure of code coverage?

A. Use-case coverage
B. Decision coverage
C. Boundary value
D. Equivalence partition coverage

APPROACHES TO TESTING

There are many ways to test a software component or system, including approaches such as static testing, dynamic testing, scripted testing and unscripted testing. These approaches may be alternatives in some cases, but they may be used together to enhance the effectiveness of testing in other situations.

Static testing

Static testing is the term used for testing a component or system at specification or code level without execution of the software.

Static testing is the only testing option before code is executed. It can be used to test the suitability of a specification to its intended purpose (reviews), and it can be used on source code to check conformance to specified rules (static analysis).

Reviews can of course also be carried out on test strategies, plans and scripts – these are not dependent on code execution.

The benefit of static testing is the detection of defects as early in the life cycle as possible, where they should be cheaper to fix, as well as reducing the possibility of fault multiplication downstream.

Dynamic testing and analysis

Dynamic testing and analysis involves execution of the software under test. It seeks to uncover defects in the system while it is running.

Dynamic analysis helps to detect defects at coding level, such as memory leaks while the code is running.

Scripted testing

A scripted test is one for which the test steps and expected results have been derived and documented (scripted) before the test is actually run. This has the advantage that all tests are repeatable and required levels of coverage can be designed into the tests. The scripts provide evidence of the testing performed.

A disadvantage is that tests cannot exploit weaknesses found during testing (unless additional scripts are written). If they are based on structured techniques they may not identify defects arising from random effects such as those that typically arise from human error.

Unscripted testing

Unscripted testing, as its name suggests, is one where a test has not been scripted fully before execution. This approach to testing is common when using experience-based techniques such as error guessing and exploratory testing.

In error guessing, a list of errors may be produced prior to test execution. In exploratory testing, the tester explores system behaviour at will, but the test steps should be recorded for future use, especially if a defect is detected.

One benefit of unscripted testing is that it can be seen as less tedious than scripted testing, in that time does not have to be spent on documenting tests before execution. It also allows the tester to explore 'what if?' scenarios.

Disadvantages include lack of repeatability and traceability back to the specifications.

FUNDAMENTALS OF TEST ANALYSIS AND TEST DESIGN

The fundamental test analysis and design process is shown in Figure 5.1.

Here we see that test analysis begins with the analysis of the test basis in order to identify the test objectives (or test conditions and test scenarios).

It continues with the selection of suitable test design techniques for the test conditions and identification of appropriate test coverage measures (usually governed by the choice of test design technique). From this a set of test cases is produced.

It finishes with the creation of manual or automated test scripts ready for execution.

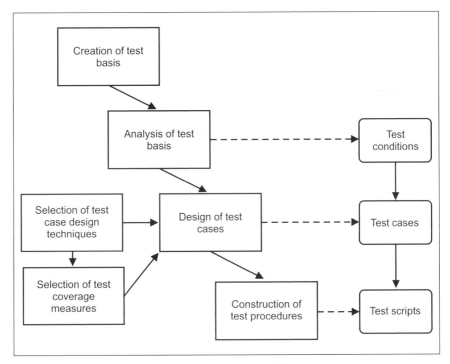

FIGURE 5.1   *The test analysis and design process*

TEST CONDITION

An item or event of a component or system that could be verified by one or more test cases, for example a function, transaction, feature, quality attribute or structural element.

Creation of a test basis

A test basis is the set of requirements against which tests are constructed. A test basis is not always a well-constructed requirements document and, in many cases, no written specification of requirements is available. In such cases a written specification of some kind must be constructed so that test conditions can be extracted and used to construct test cases and test scripts.

TEST BASIS

All documents from which the requirements of a component or system can be inferred. The documentation on which the test cases are based.

A test basis may be constructed from existing documentation, such as a user manual for an earlier version of the system or from documents used to explore requirements, including relevant emails, memos or other fragments of information. Document fragments can be validated and expanded on by conversations, formal or informal, with representatives from the user or developer communities, and it is particularly important to obtain the tacit approval of at least one significant stakeholder from the user community for any constructed test basis.

A test basis must be suitable for the extraction of test conditions, thus the best guide to the adequacy of a test basis is the construction of a set of test conditions; the exercise will highlight any weaknesses of definition in the test basis and may identify gaps in the requirements.

Analysis of a test basis

The analysis of a test basis is a very important step in the overall test analysis and design process for two reasons:

- Analysis identifies the test conditions that form the definition of the test basis from which tests will be constructed.
- Analysis recognises where the test basis is not adequately defined to enable unambiguous and complete test conditions to be identified, and thus contributes to enhancing the quality of the test basis.

The most important attribute of a test condition is that it can be verified by one or more test cases. Any requirement in the test basis for which a test condition cannot be constructed that is capable of being verified by one or more test cases is usually regarded as being inadequately defined. These are usually referred back to the business for clarification.

A test condition must therefore be unambiguous and explicit, and must contain a definition of the means by which it will be verified. This may be a measure of success, such as a performance specification or a criterion for acceptance of the defined function. Without this level of definition the requirement will be open to interpretation, and the possibility of different interpretations by developers and testers must be recognised. This state of affairs, where a test indicates failure to meet a requirement when the development team believe the requirement has been met, creates the risk of disagreement and the subsequent rework that would follow on from investigation of any discrepancies.

The test professional's task is to identify test conditions from requirements and document them, highlighting any areas of uncertainty or ambiguity to the requirements authority.

Generation of test cases

TEST CASE

A set of input values, execution preconditions, expected results and execution postconditions, developed for a particular objective or test condition, such as to exercise a particular program path or to verify compliance with a specific requirement.

Test cases are created from test conditions by application of suitable test design techniques. Selection of test design techniques and coverage measures are explored in detail on pages 129–140. Test cases identify the nature of the inputs and expected results needed to verify a given test condition, and so form the framework for test scripts. A test case identifies the nature and range of inputs and the relationship between inputs and expected outputs, the required preconditions for a test, and the relationship between preconditions and postconditions of the test. Test scripts then apply specific test data and the necessary test procedure to create a test.

Construction of test procedures

TEST PROCEDURE SPECIFICATION

A document specifying a sequence of actions for the execution of a test. Also known as test script or manual test script.

A test procedure, or test script, contains the sequence of actions needed for the execution of a single test. A test script may be run once or many times with each run using a different data set. In some cases the tests may be progressive, so that the postconditions of one test match the preconditions for the next test. Thus, provided the test environment remains unchanged, a sequence of test scripts can be run to test a complete set of related activities. Sequencing of the test scripts is the role of the test execution schedule. Both the test script(s) and the test execution schedule can be automated.

The foregoing text has pointed to the significance of defining test preconditions and postconditions in a test script. Test procedures will normally be constructed with efficiency in mind, so the opportunity to identify and implement sequences of tests, tests that progressively update a database, or tests that cycle around a particular control structure to test alternative conditions, is valuable and justifies the effort of defining preconditions and postconditions.

AUTOMATED SCRIPTING TECHNIQUES

Data-driven testing

A scripting technique stores test input and expected results in a table or spreadsheet, so that a single control script can execute all of the tests in the table. Data-driven testing is often used to support the application of test execution tools such as capture/playback tools.

Keyword-driven testing

A scripting technique that uses data files to contain not only test data and expected results, but also keywords related to the application being tested. The keywords are interpreted by special supporting scripts that are called by the control script for the test.

Test environment requirements

The purpose of a test environment is to facilitate the successful execution of a test, and at the intended level.

Thus, at unit and integration test levels, the test environment would be expected to include the necessary test harnesses, stubs and drivers.

At system test level, the environment would be expected to facilitate end-to-end testing. This may include use of machines with different operating systems and capacities, creation of large amounts of data, creation of multi-tiered architectures and use of different browsers.

At acceptance test level the test environment may be required to be as 'like live' as possible. This may necessitate the creation of a 'model office', mimicking the real office environment as much as possible.

TEST ENVIRONMENT

An environment containing hardware, instrumentation, simulators, software tools and other support elements needed to conduct a test.

CHECK OF UNDERSTANDING CU1 – TEST ENVIRONMENT REQUIREMENTS

Which of the following best describes the purpose of a test environment?

A. To ensure that all stubs and drivers are available for unit and integration testing.

B. To ensure that all data copied from the live environment has been made anonymous.

C. To ensure that the testers can carry out testing as quickly as possible.

D. To facilitate the testing of a component or system against its requirements.

EXERCISE 1 – TEST ANALYSIS ACTIVITIES

Which of the following would be included in test analysis?

i.   Creation of a specification document.

ii. Creation of test cases.

iii. Creation of test procedures.

iv. Unit testing of the code.

v.   Fixing of a defect.

A. i and ii

B. ii and iii

C. iii and iv

D. iv and v

TEST DESIGN TECHNIQUES AND TEST TYPES

Principles of test design techniques

Test design techniques provide a structured way of creating test cases that can be both effective and efficient. Effectiveness is achieved by constructing techniques around fundamental principles of testing to ensure that testing is directed first to the areas where defects are most likely to be found. Boundary value analysis, met in the Foundation syllabus, is an example of exploiting the principle that errors cluster around boundaries. Efficiency is achieved by defining techniques that exploit the structure of the software under test to minimise the number of test cases required to achieve a given level of coverage; equivalence partitioning is an example that exploits the fact that one single item of input data in a given (suitably defined) partition can achieve as much as any larger group of data items (in the same partition) in identifying defects.

Categories of test design techniques

Test design techniques fall into three main categories: specification-based, structure-based and experience-based. Specification-based and experience-based techniques, taken together, are collectively known as black-box techniques; structure-based techniques are known as white-box techniques.

Specification-based techniques are those that use the specifications as the test basis. In the V model, these would include the program, technical, functional and requirement specifications.

Some specification-based techniques are defined in BS7925-2 Sections 5.1 to 5.5. The classification tree method and use case testing need to be added to that list, and still others could be added, such as requirements-based testing.

Requirements-based testing tests each requirement in a requirements specification. This may overlap with other specification-based techniques in many cases but it will also include tests derived directly from the test condition(s) and not using any of the other specification-based techniques. Structure-based techniques are those which use a structural definition of the system, such as flow charts or call-tree diagrams. Most commonly, however, the test cases are derived from the source code. They include all those defined in BS7925-2 Sections 5.6 to 5.12. Note that structure-based techniques are applicable to any structure, including such products as user menu structures and work (business) processes.

Experience-based techniques are all those based on the experience of the testers or others to derive test cases. These include error guessing and exploratory testing.

Test design techniques

Test design techniques were introduced in the Foundation syllabus and the Intermediate syllabus adds no new techniques.

However, if you passed the Foundation Certificate examination some time ago you will need to be familiar with techniques introduced into the Foundation syllabus in recent years (circa 2006). This section provides a brief recap of the techniques you will need to be familiar with.

Specification-based techniques

Specification-based techniques are those that use written specifications as the test basis. In the V model, written specifications might be expected at the requirements specification, functional specification, design and coding levels. In an iterative life cycle model written specifications are less likely to be produced, except at the beginning of a timebox, when requirements are at least outlined.

The specification-based test case design techniques introduced in the ISEB Foundation syllabus were:

- equivalence partitioning
- boundary value analysis
- decision table testing
- state transition testing
- use case testing.

For all except use case testing you should be able to design test cases using the technique, though you will not be examined on this aspect at Intermediate level. Definitions of most of the techniques and worked examples in the design of test cases can be found in BS7925-2.

Specification-based techniques are also known as black-box techniques. The term 'black box' relates to the idea that these techniques treat a specification as something that defines the outputs that will be generated for given inputs, that is they treat the system built from a specification as a black box and take no interest in how the outputs are generated.

Equivalence partitioning

Equivalence partitioning uses the specification to identify partitions (groups of inputs or outputs) that are equivalent in the sense that all inputs in an input partition produce a common output and all outputs in an output partition arise from a given input. It is based on the idea that every input or output in a partition is equivalent and therefore a test of any one is equally valid and representative of the entire partition.

Normally at least one test case is selected for each partition. These test cases are often augmented by test cases derived by boundary value analysis.

Boundary value analysis

Boundary value analysis uses the specification to determine the boundaries of each input or output partition. Values just inside and just outside the boundary can then be tested to ensure that the partition boundary is in the correct place. The most common form of boundary value analysis would use two values, one of which is valid (i.e. on or inside the boundary) and the other not valid (outside the boundary). By selecting values as close as possible to the specified boundary the location of the actual boundary can be determined accurately. There is an alternative that uses three boundary values: one just inside the boundary; one on the boundary; and one just outside the boundary.

Boundary value analysis exploits the principle that defects tend to cluster at boundaries. It is a natural partner to equivalence partitioning since it uses the same partitions and adds test cases to those already defined by equivalence partitioning.

Decision table testing

Decision table testing is used for testing systems for which the specification takes the form of rules or cause-effect combinations. In a decision table the inputs (causes) are listed in a column, with the outputs (effects) in the same column but below the inputs. The remainder of the table explores combinations of inputs to define the outputs produced. Thus each column of the table represents rules or combinations of inputs and the outputs produced. A decision table may capture all input combinations or it may be limited to those that are feasible or relevant, in which case the table is known as a limited entry decision table.

A decision table may be constructed from a cause-effect graph, though this is not a requirement of the technique.

State transition testing

State transition testing is used for systems whose behaviour is defined in terms of states and events. A system can rest in any of a number of states defined in the specification and will change from one state to another when a given event occurs. Events are also documented in the specification. A state transition diagram captures the states and events, showing how valid combinations of states and events generate system behaviour. State transition testing designs test cases to exercise valid transitions and, where appropriate, ensure that correct outputs are generated.

Use case testing

Use case testing takes a specification defined in terms of use cases, each representing a single user interaction with the system, and designs test cases to test each use case.

Structure-based techniques

Structure-based techniques are those that apply when detailed information about how the software was constructed is available as a basis for deriving test cases.

The structure-based test case design techniques introduced in Foundation were:

- statement testing
- decision testing.

You should be able to generate test cases with either of these techniques though, as for specification-based techniques, you will not be examined on this aspect at Intermediate level. As for specification-based techniques, definitions of the techniques and worked examples in the use of the techniques can be found in BS7925-2.

Structure-based techniques are also known as white-box techniques. The term 'white-box' relates to the idea that the structure of the system is visible. White-box techniques focus attention on how outputs are generated from given inputs by tracing the system's internal behaviour.

Statement testing

Statement testing uses program source code to design test cases that exercise every executable program statement in a program. Executable statements include all statements except those used to set aside (declare) working space for the program, and any blank lines or comment lines within the source code.

Decision testing

Decision testing uses program source code to design test cases that exercise every decision outcome in a program. Thus at every branch point in a program's structure where the next step is determined by the value of a Boolean variable (i.e. one that can have the values 'True' or 'False' only) the program must be executed for the case when the variable has the value 'True' and the case when the variable has the value 'False'.

Experience-based techniques

The experience-based design techniques introduced in the ISEB Foundation syllabus were:

- error guessing
- exploratory testing.

Experience-based techniques are also known as black-box techniques, together with specification-based techniques.

Experience-based techniques use the knowledge and experience of users, testers or developers to generate test cases based on likely areas of failure.

Error guessing

Error guessing is a test case design technique that relies on the experience of the tester to select appropriate test cases to exploit weaknesses of the software under test. The test cases may be based on checklists of typical failures or on more sophisticated analyses of past failure modes, as in a fault attack.

Exploratory testing

Exploratory testing uses the results of tests to design new tests so that a tester can explore weaknesses in detail. The approach is managed by defining an overall mission and by timeboxing test sessions in a manner similar to iterative development methods.

Benefits and pitfalls of test design techniques

The benefits of test design techniques stem from the fact that each technique has been designed for a specific kind of software specification or structure:

- State transition testing is applicable to state-based systems (examples include systems with switching mechanisms, such as gears in a car, traffic lights, televisions etc.).
- Use case testing works for systems defined by use cases; often in iterative development environments.
- Decision table testing is most effective when applied to rule-based systems (such as billing systems and retail insurance schemes).

Others are more generally applicable: equivalence partitioning and boundary value analysis can, in principle, be applied to any system. Boundary value analysis is particularly well suited to any system in which boundaries are clearly evident.

Here, then, is an important stumbling block. Requirements are not always written in a way that facilitates (or even enables) the use of structured test design techniques. This is the main reason why use of the techniques demands so much skill. Testers are more likely to fall back on business domain knowledge to define and prioritise tests if the application of structured techniques takes longer and is more error prone, which is often the case in practice.

Table 5.1 shows the benefits and pitfalls of using techniques.

TABLE 5.1   *The benefits and pitfalls of test design techniques*

Benefits	Pitfalls
Efficient testing – fewer resources used and faster completion of testing than for an unstructured testing approach.	Requirements are not always written to facilitate structured testing, leading to dependence on business domain knowledge.
Cost-effective testing – fewer test cases to achieve a desired level of risk reduction.	Techniques do not suit all types of requirement.
Measured achievement of risk reduction – measures of coverage can be directly related to risk.	Testers need considerable skill and experience to make techniques effective.

Criteria for selecting test design techniques

Given that there are both benefits and pitfalls in using structured test design techniques, some criteria for making an appropriate selection are essential.

The key criteria used for selection will be those that characterise the nature of the application under test and the nature of the test design technique:

- Safety critical applications require the specific test design techniques defined in the relevant safety critical standard; in general, these will include both specification-based and structure-based techniques with associated coverage measures.
- Test design techniques must be appropriate to the nature of the application (e.g. state transition testing is appropriate to state-based systems).
- Specification-based test design techniques are appropriate to any application for which an adequate specification exists.
- Structure-based test design techniques are appropriate to any code but, in general, the cost of extensive testing at this level will only be justified for relatively high risk or high value applications.
- Structure-based test design techniques are always applicable to structures other than code (e.g. menu structures).
- Structure-based test design techniques are most appropriate to the component test level and the early stages of integration testing, after which the complexity of integrated components generally becomes too high for the techniques to be practicable.
- Experience-based test design techniques are applicable as the primary means of defining tests where no adequate specification exists from which to derive specification-based tests, and may be appropriate in other circumstances, but they are seldom appropriate as the primary means of generating tests where some formal record of testing is required.

- Structured test design techniques should only be deployed where testing staff are trained and capable of using them effectively.
- Specific test design techniques may be mandated in a test strategy or a test policy, in which case an organisation is accepting responsibility for maintaining the ability to deploy the techniques effectively.

This list of criteria is neither systematic nor exhaustive but covers the majority of practical cases that will be encountered.

Test types

Test types are defined as groups of test activities that focus on a specific test objective. So far we have considered test design techniques that contribute to the functional testing test type. We have also earlier considered regression testing, confirmation testing and other test types as they have arisen in the discussion of testing in the life cycle. Test types can occur at all levels.

One important test type that we have not discussed yet is the non-functional test type. The testing of non-functional attributes can be challenging, and a collection of test techniques have been developed to tackle the complexities of areas such as performance testing, usability testing, reliability testing and many other important areas.

The selection of non-functional test types is beyond the scope of the Intermediate syllabus and will not be dealt with in detail in this book, but a broad knowledge of test types and the selection of appropriate test types is the hallmark of a good tester.

In the context of the Intermediate syllabus, selection of non-functional test types is not a major concern because non-functional tests are invariably directed specifically at the non-functional attributes they are designed to test. Effective application of selected test types is taken up in the Test Analysis Practitioner syllabus.

EXERCISE 2 – SELECTION OF TEST DESIGN TECHNIQUES

1. Match each description on the left to the activity on the right.

i. A tester finding errors in a functional specification	p. Static testing
ii. A developer finding faults when his code is running	q. Dynamic testing
iii. A developer finding errors in source code	
iv. A tester finding that a feature does not work	

A. i–p, ii–p, iii–q, iv–q
B. i–p, ii–q, iii–p, iv–q

     C. i–q, ii–q, iii–q, iv–q
     D. i–q, ii–p, iii–q, iv–p

2. Match the situation on the left to the best recommended test approach on the right:

---

i. Safety critical system	m. Scripted testing
ii. Specifications available	n. Unscripted testing
iii. Testers know how the system should work	
iv. Existing system is being migrated onto a new platform	

     A. i–m, ii–m, iii–n, iv–n
     B. i–n, ii–n, iii–m, iv–m
     C. i–m, ii–n, iii–m, iv–n
     D. i–n, ii–m, iii–n, iv–m

3. Which of the following best describes the purpose of formal test case design techniques?

     A. They allow systems to be tested as efficiently as possible.
     B. They allow early visibility of the test process to be followed.
     C. They allow the project manager to understand the time required to conduct proper testing.
     D. They allow the test basis to be systematically tested.

4. Match the test technique on the left to its category on the right:

---

i. State transition testing	r. Specification-based
ii. Decision table testing	s. Structure-based
iii. Decision testing	t. Experience-based
iv. Exploratory testing	
v. Error guessing	
vi. Path testing	

     A. ii and iii – r, i and iv – s, v and vi – t
     B. i and iii – r, ii and vi – s, iv and v – t
     C. i and ii – r, iii and vi – s, iv and v – t
     D. ii and vi – r, iii and iv – s, i and iii – t

TEST COVERAGE

Principles of test coverage

Test coverage is a way of setting the desired extent of testing to reduce risk to a given acceptable level. So test coverage is a way of defining the extent of testing and is usually driven by the level of risk that needs to be mitigated.

> ### TEST COVERAGE
>
> The degree, expressed as a percentage, to which a specified coverage item has been exercised by a test suite.

Coverage items can be anything for which coverage can be measured. Boundary values and equivalence partitions (EP) have already been mentioned and each of these has a coverage measure.

The EP coverage measure would be

$$\frac{\text{Number of equivalence partitions exercised by a test suite}}{\text{Total number of equivalence partitions}}$$

Note that the definition is in terms of test suites rather than test cases; the coverage achieved by a test case can be aggregated to the level of test suites, where all partitions exercised more than once are counted as if they had been tested once, and all partitions tested by any of the test cases are also counted as tested once. The general definition of coverage can be extended to almost all of the test design techniques to measure coverage of functionality or structure.

Test coverage measures

Coverage measures play a vital role in testing as a risk reduction activity because coverage measures provide an important link between testing and exit criteria. Exit criteria are the means by which acceptable risk at any test level is defined. Without coverage measures the quality and extent of testing are open to interpretation and subject to the usual pressures of time and resources.

The test coverage measures introduced in Foundation were:

- statement coverage
- decision coverage.

These coverage measures apply to the structure-based techniques and you should be aware that there are more sophisticated measures of coverage that could be adopted. There are also coverage measures associated with specification-based techniques and all these measures are defined in BS7925-2, where you will also find worked examples.

Statement coverage

Statement coverage is defined as the percentage of executable statements exercised by a test suite. Executable statements are all the statements in a program other than those (normally at the beginning of a program) that set aside storage. Such statements are known as declarations. In a program listing we would count all statements other than declarations and comment lines, and we would ignore any blank lines in the program listing that may have been included as formatting.

When the program is run we count all the statements that are executed and calculate what percentage of executable statements has been exercised. Where a test suite contains multiple tests the total coverage achieved by all tests would be the measure of statement coverage.

Note that determining which statements have been executed at run time requires a means of monitoring the program's behaviour. This is usually done by means of instrumentation, which is a technique that adds statements to a program to monitor behaviour.

Decision coverage

Decision coverage is defined as the percentage of decision outcomes that have been exercised by a test suite. It is measured in a similar way to statement coverage, except that in this case we monitor decision outcomes by determining each occasion when the 'True' outcome of a decision is exercised and each time a 'False' outcome is exercised.

Other coverage measures

The idea of coverage can be applied to any well-defined aspect of a system under test, including non-functional aspects; we could define requirements coverage, user interface coverage, rule coverage or any coverage measure relevant to the nature of the system under test, provided only that the measure is well defined and useful in determining the extent of testing.

Coverage measures and risk

> **RISK**
>
> A factor that could result in future negative consequences; usually expressed as impact and likelihood.

The definition of risk leaves a clear avenue for effective risk reduction: remove the factors that will have a negative impact or reduce the likelihood of their occurrence. For every product risk there is a link between the occurrence of the risk factor and testing, which is why testing is commonly based on risk. A risk-based testing strategy targets identified risks as the main thrust of testing. The question that remains, however, is whether enough testing has been done to eliminate the risk.

There is no absolute answer to that question because the effect of testing depends on how effectively the risk was targeted in the test design, but we can at least get some measure of whether the testing has covered all areas of the system or all areas where a given risk is anticipated to arise. This is the function of coverage measures; they give assurance that the coverage of system requirements, system functionality or system structure is at the desired level. Exit criteria set the level of desired coverage, coverage analysis measures achieved coverage, and test design constructs tests to achieve desired coverage.

COVERAGE ANALYSIS

Measurement of achieved coverage to a specified coverage item during test execution referring to predetermined criteria to find out whether additional testing is required and, if so, which test cases are needed.

Benefits and pitfalls of coverage measures

The benefits of coverage have already been identified but are worth repeating. Coverage measures provide objective evidence of the achievement of a given level of coverage and this, in turn, points to the quality of testing and the extent of risk reduction.

The pitfalls are more subtle. The link between coverage and quality is not absolute and not guaranteed, and coverage does not automatically affect the likelihood of a risk factor occurring. A collection of tests that exercises every function but with tests that have little probability of finding defects is not an effective test suite; likewise a collection of tests directed at an area of the system where a risk factor has been identified but not correctly directed at the risk factor may achieve an exit criterion but not reduce risk. The examples, though, are somewhat fanciful. Would a tester apply the considerable effort required to achieve a measured level of coverage and not pay attention to the quality of the tests? Is the ability to construct a suite of tests to achieve a measured level of coverage consistent with not correctly targeting the tests?

A more likely pitfall arises from the sheer cost and time it takes to apply coverage rigorously. These are sufficiently prohibitive that coverage measurement is rare outside those environments where it is mandatory. The problem lies in the nature of coverage. The hard fact is that no level of coverage provides any confidence that a system meets its requirements, and this is the single most important risk factor that testing is intended to remove or reduce.

The most effective use of coverage measures is to first ensure adequate functional coverage by use of appropriate specification-based coverage measures. When all planned functional testing has been completed a measure of structural coverage achieved can be used to decide whether further testing is justified, in which case structure-based tests can be defined to increase structural coverage to an acceptable level.

Practical coverage measurement

In practical situations coverage measurement will be appropriate whenever coverage is used as an entry or exit criterion for a test level. This will be most often for safety critical or other high-risk applications.

Functional coverage measures (i.e. those associated with specification-based test design techniques) can be incorporated into entry and exit criteria for system and acceptance testing to ensure that coverage of functionality is adequate before an application is released.

Structural coverage measures may be used informally at the component testing level and incorporated into exit criteria from component testing to provide confidence that adequate testing has been carried out on components before integration begins. In this case the criteria would typically be limited to statement and decision coverage at levels that could be achieved without the use of coverage measurement tools; the criteria set would then depend on the complexity of code components. Cyclomatic complexity could, in such cases, also be used as a quality measure for code components, with components that have a complexity above a certain value being exposed to a code inspection before component testing or before release to the next testing level.

One practical consideration is the need for instrumentation to measure coverage achieved. Instrumentation involves modifying the system under test to enable the execution of structural elements (such as statements and decisions) to be counted at test run time. This modification to the system under test may not be acceptable. In any event it is an expensive exercise and the instrumentation will need to be carefully removed after testing. Some level of regression testing will also be needed to confirm that the instrumentation has been completely removed and the system has been returned to its normal state.

> **CHECK OF UNDERSTANDING CU2 – COVERAGE MEASURES**
>
> Which of the following are test coverage measures and which are test progress measures?
>
> A. Percentage of equivalence partitions tested.
> B. Percentage of decisions tested.
> C. Percentage of tests passed.
> D. Percentage of statements tested.

SCENARIO ANALYSIS

The analysis of a scenario to identify suitable test case design techniques and test coverage measures is a key skill for the Intermediate examination and for your competence as a test analyst. This is an area of testing skill that will be addressed again and developed further by the Test Analysis Practitioner syllabus.

For the Intermediate examination the most important skill is to be able to recognise the key characteristics of a scenario and to make an optimum choice of technique or coverage measure from the alternatives available. This can be a difficult judgement to make in reality but in the examination the scenario will be constrained to enable you to make a rational selection from the information available, so it is a matter of recognising what is most significant and using that to make a selection.

As a simple example, safety critical systems invariably require the use of specification-based techniques with associated coverage measures. In any scenario involving safety critical systems that will be the most significant factor driving choice of techniques and coverage measures. In other scenarios the nature of the application may be state-based and this will point towards state transition testing. In the real world there may be a number of such pointers that conflict with each other and judgement may be difficult; in an Intermediate examination this will not be the case and the factors driving your selection will be clear as long as you are able to analyse the scenario to discover what they are.

EXERCISE 3 – SCENARIO ANALYSIS

Scenario

An air traffic control system monitors aircraft in flight.

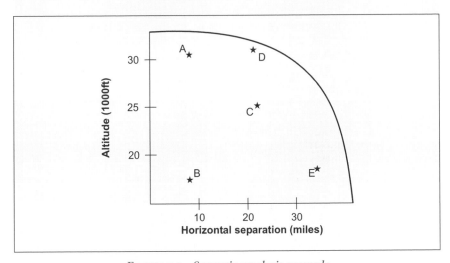

FIGURE 5.2 *Scenario analysis example*

The diagram shows a representative display showing five aircraft in flight (A–E).

The arc represents the controller's field of view. Aircraft in this view are under his control. Aircraft outside this range are shown on other controllers' displays.

The rules for managing aircraft in flight are as follows.

When aircraft are within 5 miles of the same horizontal position, safe vertical separation between aircraft is considered to be 1,000 ft (305 m) at altitudes below 29,000 ft (8,845 m), and 2,000 ft (610 m) at altitudes of 29,000 ft and above. When aircraft are at the same altitude (i.e. within 1,000 ft below 29,000 ft and within 2,000 ft at 29,000 ft or above), safe horizontal separation is considered to be 5 miles (8 km).

Aircraft that are in immediate danger of conflicting with safety distances are shown with a flashing symbol on the screen. The controller then directs the pilot to alter aircraft position accordingly to maintain safe distances.

1. Which of the following accurately reflects the requirements above?
   A. Safe vertical separation will be 1,000 ft for altitudes of 29,000 ft.
   B. Safe horizontal separation will be 8 km for altitudes of 29,000 ft or above.
   C. Safe vertical separation will be 305 m for altitudes below 8,845 m.
   D. Safe vertical separation will be 2,000 ft at altitudes of 29,000 ft and above.

2. Which of the following test design techniques would be best suited to check correct display of aircraft, according to the rules specified?
   A. Boundary value analysis
   B. Path testing
   C. Decision testing
   D. Use case testing

3. Which of the following test design techniques would be best suited to check that the code can be fully executed?
   A. Boundary value analysis
   B. Decision testing
   C. Statement testing
   D. State transition testing

SUMMARY

The main purpose of this part of the syllabus and this chapter is to extend knowledge of test design techniques from their use in designing test cases to their effective deployment in a given practical situation. This is directly related to the management of testing through the use of measures to determine how testing is progressing towards its quality objectives.

The first topic we addressed was the fundamentals of test analysis, the basic elements on which all test design is based, irrespective of the techniques used. Allied to this is the definition of test environment, and we discussed the nature of test environment requirements.

The largest part of this chapter is devoted to the understanding and selection of the many test design techniques that can be used in creating tests. The categorisation of techniques and the definition of objective criteria for selection of techniques, including the coverage measures associated with them, are of central importance, and a clear understanding of the benefits and pitfalls of individual techniques is essential to good judgements about technique and coverage measure selection. The skill of analysing situations in order to make appropriate decisions is fundamental and opportunities to practice this skill are provided through exercises.

There is a mind map of this chapter in Appendix A.

EXAMPLE EXAMINATION QUESTIONS

Scenario

An internet service provider (ISP) offers its services mainly to home users. With this group, a major target is home users with children. One of its key selling points is its Parental Control (PC) system. The PC system allows the user with Master rights to set the internet access privileges of the other users. Its categories of user are: Mature Teen (M), General Teen (G), Kids only (KO).

- A Mature Teen can have 24-hour access, can access websites in the M category and can visit chat rooms.
- A General Teen can have '9–5' access, can access websites in the G category and can visit chat rooms.
- A Kid can have access up to 1 hour per day, can access websites in the KO category only, but cannot visit chat rooms.

E1

Which of the following provides the best description of a test condition for this system?

A. The system will allow a user to have Master rights.
B. The system will allow a General Teen to have 24-hour access.
C. The system will allow Kids access to the M category of websites.
D. The system will allow a Mature Teen to access only specified chat rooms.

E2

Which of the following test design techniques would be best suited to testing that a General Teen can have only '9–5' access to the system?

A. State transition testing
B. Equivalence partitioning
C. Path testing
D. Statement testing

E3

Which of the following types of testing would be best suited to checking the source code for data flow errors?

A. Static analysis
B. Dynamic analysis
C. Performance testing
D. Boundary value analysis

E4

For which of the following would decision testing be most suited?

A. To check that the system allows the creation of a Master user.
B. To check that the Master user can set access privileges.
C. To check that the code relating to the Master user can be fully executed.
D. To check that the Master user can be changed to a different user.

ANSWERS TO SELF-ASSESSMENT QUESTIONS (ON PAGES 120–121)

SA1. B
SA2. A
SA3. B

ANSWERS TO CHECKS OF UNDERSTANDING

CU1 (on page 126)

The correct answer is D. Here is the reasoning.

Answer A will form part of the test environment, but is applicable only at the lower levels of testing.

Answer B, once again, is relevant, but is just one part (if required) of a test environment.

Answer C may be important, but is not usually a consideration when designing a test environment.

Answer D refers to the whole of the test activity, which provides the best answer for the purpose of a test environment.

CU2 (on page 138)

Answers A, B and D are test quality measures, while answer C is a test progress measure.

ANSWERS TO EXERCISES

Exercise 1 (on page 127)

The correct answer is B. Here is the reasoning.

Option i refers to the creation of specification. This is part of system design, not testing.

Option ii refers to creating a test asset, therefore it is part of test analysis.

Option iii, again, is applicable to the test effort, therefore is part of test analysis.

Option iv refers to unit testing, this is test execution, not analysis.

Option v refers to fixing a defect, part of the development activity, not testing.

Thus options ii and iii are correct.

Exercise 2 (on page 133)

1. The correct answer is B. Here is the reasoning.

    Static testing refers to testing conducted on work products not involving the execution of code. This applies to specifications and source code – descriptions i and iii.

    Dynamic testing refers to testing done on code that is being executed. This applies to developers conducting testing on code that is being executed, and testers checking that features work as expected – descriptions ii and iv.

2. The correct answer is A. Here is the reasoning.

    Scripted testing is the ideal, in all situations. For safety critical systems it is essential (situation i). It should also be used when specifications are available (situation ii).

    Unscripted testing does have its place, and can be used to capitalise on tester knowledge. It can be used to complement the scripted testing effort. It is often used when specifications are not available, but we do have some understanding of how the system should work (situation iii). An example of this is when an existing system has been migrated onto a different platform (situation iv).

3. The correct answer is D. Here is the reasoning.

    Answer A suggests an efficiency gain by making use of formal techniques. While this may be a benefit, it is by no means assured. Efficiency depends on other factors such as tester skill etc.

    Answer B, the test process, encompasses much more than test design, which is just one part of the process. Using test design techniques will allow visibility of how test procedures have been created, not the whole test process.

    Answer C could be a benefit, but again, this option focuses on just one aspect of testing. Other factors from a project management perspective would include time required for setting up the test environment, executing tests and analysing results.

    Answer D is the primary purpose of a formal test design technique, and thus is the best answer.

4. The correct answer is C. Here is the reasoning:

    Specification-based (or black-box techniques) include:

- Equivalence partitioning
- Boundary value analysis
- State transition testing
- Decision table testing
- Use case testing

Options i and ii from the table are applicable.

Structure-based (or white-box techniques) include:

- Statement testing
- Decision testing
- Condition testing
- Path testing

Options iii and vi from the table are applicable.

Experience-based techniques include:

- Error guessing
- Exploratory testing

Options iv and v from the table are applicable.

Thus the correct answer is C.

Exercise 3 (on page 139)

1. The best answer is D. Answers A–C do not match the requirements given.

2. The best answer is A. Options B and C are structure-based techniques, which will test the code but cannot determine whether it meets the rules of the specification. Option D could be used if the rules formed part of a use case definition, but the nature of the application and the precision of the safety-related rules point to a technique that can determine that the rules have been correctly implemented. Boundary value analysis is most appropriate because it enables the key boundaries to be explicitly tested.

3. The best answer is B. Options A and D are specification-based techniques, used to test conformance to the specification, but not that the code correctly reflects safety distances. Screen resolution would not allow accurate measurement of the distances when controllers are alerted but the values in the code can be exercised directly with a structure-based technique and decision testing could be used to ensure that all decisions leading to an alert to the controller are correctly programmed. Option C is a structure-based technique, but is not as thorough in testing for code execution as decision testing is.

ANSWERS TO EXAMPLE EXAMINATION QUESTIONS

E1 (on page 141)

The correct answer is A. Answers B–D do not match the scenario described.

Answer B – General Teens should have '9–5' access.

Answer C – Kids should have access to the KO category of websites only.

Answer D – The specification is not clear on whether all chat rooms should be available to Mature Teens. This would need to be clarified.

E2 (on page 141)

The correct answer is B.

Answer A – State transition testing is best suited to state-based systems.

Answer C – Path testing is a white-box testing technique. It will test that all paths through the code can be executed, not that the outcomes are as defined in the specifications.

Answer D – The statement is also a white-box technique. It will check that every executable statement can be executed, but as for path testing, not that the outcome is correct against the specification.

E3 (on page 142)

The correct answer is A.

Answer B – Dynamic analysis is used to test the code, while it is running, for defects such as memory leaks.

Answer C – Performance testing is used on software that is running, checking for issues with loading.

Answer D – Boundary value analysis is also used on software that is running, to check for defects around defined boundaries.

E4 (on page 142)

The correct answer is C.

Answers A, B and D are related to the system definition, they would be tested using black-box techniques. Answer C relates to the code itself, and would be tested by a white-box technique, such as decision testing.

6 The examination

INTRODUCTION

The Intermediate Certificate examination has a very important role; it acts as a bridge between the relatively straightforward Foundation examination, with questions up to the K3 level, and the much more challenging essay style of the Practitioner Certificate examinations, which are at levels up to K6.

In this progression, the single most difficult step that candidates have found in the past is that from K3 to K4, and the reason is that K4 requires the skill of applying knowledge in a realistic context. The Intermediate syllabus therefore concentrates on the analysis skill, adding relatively little new technical information to what was specified for Foundation. The focus at Intermediate is on adding depth to the understanding of core topics so that they can be applied effectively to real-life situations. The K4 learning objectives signal the need to be able to analyse a scenario and apply the theoretical ideas in the syllabus to the context of that scenario.

The ability to analyse scenarios is the single most important outcome of an Intermediate Certificate qualification, and the one that provides an effective preparation for the more advanced work at Practitioner level as well as a very important stage in the development of a testing professional.

This chapter explores the examination to identify its challenges and help you to prepare for them, providing examples so that you can see for yourself how questions are structured and how scenario analysis is used in answering them.

THE INTERMEDIATE CERTIFICATE EXAMINATION

The examination structure

The Intermediate examination is a scenario-based multiple choice examination of 25 questions that must be completed in one hour. Questions are set at levels up to K4, which require analysis of a given scenario in order to identify the correct answer.

Intermediate examination questions are all set in the context of a scenario. The questions at K1 and K2 levels will not require analysis of the scenario but will use the scenario to provide context. The K4 questions, however, will require analysis of the scenario and will not necessarily have a simple answer; the scenario may make one answer more appropriate than another in the given context. The purpose of the examination is to test candidates' ability to analyse scenarios and to apply the theory appropriately. In some questions there may be more than one answer that could be justified in the absence of any context and it is important, therefore, to apply any answer to the context before selecting it as the 'correct' option. The key to success in the Intermediate examination is the effective analysis of scenarios.

There are four main aspects to the examination's structure:

- The questions are all equally weighted.
- The number of questions at each K level will be determined from the syllabus split.
- The number of questions associated with each section of the syllabus is in proportion to the amount of time allocated to that section of the syllabus, which roughly translates into:

  Section 1 – four questions
  Section 2 – six questions
  Section 3 – four questions
  Section 4 – six questions
  Section 5 – six questions

  These proportions are approximate, which is why the total number of questions in the list above is not 25. The precise breakdown is not mandatory, but examinations will be structured along these lines and as close to these relative proportions as possible.
- The pass mark is 15 correct answers and there are no reductions for incorrect answers.

Scenarios and questions

The scenarios will be relatively brief, typically sub-divided into four paragraphs. They will contain all the details needed to enable you to answer the questions. This does not mean that the actual answers to questions will be embedded in the scenario so that all you have to do is recognise the correct answer, but it does mean that the information on which selection of the best answer depends will always be given.

Each question will contain a 'stem', which states the specific question and links back to the scenario, though the link will not necessarily always be explicit. There will always be exactly four optional responses, of which only one will be deemed the correct response. There will be no marks awarded for any response other than the correct response and there will be no reductions for any incorrect response.

Although only one of the optional answers will be correct, the remainder can be expected to be plausibly incorrect, which means that anyone knowing the correct answer will be unlikely to be drawn to any of the incorrect answers, but anyone unsure of the correct answer will be likely to find one or more alternatives plausible. It is likely that the correct answer and at least one of the incorrect answers (distracters) could be considered equally correct in the absence of the specific context embedded in the scenario, so effective analysis of the scenario is as important as knowledge of the technical content from the syllabus.

There are no absolute rules for question types as long as they are appropriate to the level of understanding they are testing, but there are some common types of question that are likely to arise. Expect to see the so-called roman style of question because it is designed to test your ability to link together relevant items of information and eliminate incorrect combinations. In the Foundation exam roman-style questions were at the K2 level; in the Intermediate exam they may be at either the K2 or the K4 level because the correct answer may depend on the context given in the scenario. Examples are provided in the next box of a scenario and typical questions at each of the K1, K2 and K4 levels. The K2 question is in the roman style.

EXAMPLE OF A SCENARIO

Games Unlimited is a small software house that builds computer games for the PC market. They have several popular games in the market. They are now embarking on a project to build their first fully interactive game to be played across the internet. The development team has been augmented for the project but the core team has built all of the previous game products.

The team will use an Agile approach to the development of the new game, with a series of timeboxes aimed at determining feasibility and product characteristics. Once these are defined the main development will aim to reuse as much as possible from existing game products. The company is hoping to achieve around 50 per cent of the product capability from reused components.

All previous products had been tested by the development team with a final acceptance test done by a group of friendly gaming enthusiasts recruited for the exercise on a part-time basis. This is not considered adequate for the new product and a testing team has been set up. You are responsible for the testing, having been recently recruited. You have so far recruited one other tester and have another vacancy to fill.

Example of a K1 question

Which one of the following review types would require a trained moderator?

A. Walkthrough
B. Management review
C. Inspection
D. Technical review

The correct answer is C. This requires only recall of the review roles and hence is a K1 question based on section 2.2 of the syllabus. There is no link to the scenario.

Example of a K2 question

Which of the following correctly describes the relationship between testing and the given life cycle model?

A. In the V model testing is planned early but not executed until development is complete.

B. In an iterative life cycle all testing is structured into test levels and detailed test specifications are prepared for each level.

C. In an iterative life cycle testing is incorporated into each timebox.

D. In a V life cycle there is no need for regression testing because the software under development is not changing.

The correct answer is C. This requires a comparison of the two life-cycle approaches and an understanding of the key testing characteristics of each. It is a K2 question based on Section 1.3 iv of the syllabus. It refers to the scenario but requires no analysis.

Example of a K4 question

In the Games Unlimited scenario above there are both product and project risks associated with the new project. Which of the following would be a product risk in this scenario?

A. The lack of experience in the new testing team could result in poor testing and subsequent poor performance of the new game.

B. The desired level of reuse might not be achieved, making the game more expensive than expected.

C. The inexperience in the testing team could result in delays from incorrect incident reports.

D. The augmented development team might find that development takes longer when working with a test team.

The correct answer is A. This is a K4 question because it requires analysis of the scenario to determine the correct answer. The question is based on Section 3.3 ii of the syllabus and requires the candidate to be able to differentiate between potential product risks and project risks in the given scenario.

The ISEB sample examination paper

The sample examination paper, which is available from ISEB, is designed to provide guidance on the structure of the paper and the 'rubric' (the rules printed on the front of the paper) of the real examination. The questions in the sample paper are not necessarily typical, though there will be examples of the various types of questions so that candidates are aware of the kinds of questions that can arise. Any topic or type of question in the sample paper can be expected to arise in a real examination at some time. The sample paper will be balanced by K level and topic weight in the syllabus. Bear in mind that the sample paper may change from time to time to reflect any changes in the syllabus or to reflect any changes in the way questions are set.

SCENARIO ANALYSIS

Scenarios present a brief context for a group of questions. Each scenario applies to more than one question, but specific details in the scenario may not be relevant to every question to which the scenario relates; only the K4 questions need analysis of the scenario. There may also be redundant information in the scenario because candidates are being asked to identify the elements of the context that are relevant and use them to select the most appropriate answer.

There is no golden rule for scenario analysis, but there are pitfalls that are easy to fall into. Here are some of these.

You will be reading many scenarios in an examination, so it is easy to confuse the details of one scenario with another scenario in your mind. As you read each scenario, making a brief summary of the main points has several benefits: it helps to make your reading 'active', which enhances understanding; the act of writing also helps to ensure that your short-term memory (your personal clipboard) overwrites its memory of the previous scenario with the details of the new one; finally, writing keeps you more alert than just reading.

When you read a familiar scenario it is easy to 'fill in' details that are not there, in much the same way as your mind completes a sentence left incomplete when someone is speaking to you. The danger here is that incompleteness in the scenario may be deliberate, and details may be deliberately left out; the reflex that 'fills in' may then lead you astray by correcting deliberate gaps in the scenario.

Another aspect of familiarity is that you may not absorb all the specific details, and this can lead you to select an incorrect option. In a multiple choice question the distracters are likely to be answers that are nearly correct but include information not supplied in the scenario, omit important information from the scenario, or distort information in the scenario. Lack of attention to key details can be disastrous in this case.

So, when you reach a scenario, pick up a pencil and give yourself a pinch to make sure you are alert, then jot down notes and check them back against the scenario. By the time you have done this you should have a good grasp of what the scenario is about. There is a good chance that when you read the scenario a second or third time you may realise that you had previously overlooked a key element. Yes, you should read a scenario two or three times;

it doesn't take long and each time you may see something that you missed previously.

PLANNING EXAMINATION REVISION

Revision techniques

There are some golden rules for exam revision.

- Do as many example questions as you can so that you become familiar with the type of questions, the way questions are worded and the levels of questions that are set in the examination.

- Be active in your reading. This usually means taking notes, but this book has been structured to include regular Checks of Understanding that will provide you with prompts to ensure you have remembered the key ideas from the section you have just revised. In many cases information you need to remember is already in note form for easy learning. Nevertheless, writing down your responses to Checks of Understanding is the best way to ensure that the information sticks.

- One important way to engage with the book is to work through all the examples and exercises. If you convince yourself you can do an exercise, but you do not actually attempt it, you will only discover your weakness when you are sitting in the examination centre.

- Learning and revision need to be reinforced. There are two related ways to do this:

  - By making structured notes to connect together related ideas. This can be done via lists, but a particularly effective way to make the connections is by using a technique known as mind mapping. An example of a mind map of the syllabus can be found in the Introduction. There are mind maps for all the chapters in Appendix A so that you can compare your attempts with ours; sometimes this can yield new insights. You can also use our mind maps as revision aids if you have not made up your own, but the learning value will be far greater if you attempt them for yourself.

  - By returning to a topic that you have revised to check that you have retained the information. This is best done the day after the time that you first revised the topic and again a week after, if possible. If you begin each revision section by returning to the Check of Understanding boxes in some or all of the chapters you worked with in previous revision sessions it will help to ensure that you retain what you are revising. Returning to mind maps made earlier will reinforce the knowledge embedded in them and potentially also refine your understanding. If you find that you update the mind maps at this stage you can be confident that you will remember that refinement.

- Read the syllabus and become familiar with it. Questions are raised directly from the syllabus and often contain wording similar to that used in the syllabus. Familiarity with the syllabus document will more than repay the time you will spend gaining that familiarity.

Examination technique

In a relatively short examination there is little time to devote to studying the paper in depth. However, it is wise to pause before beginning to answer questions while you assimilate the contents of the question paper. This brief time of inactivity is also a good opportunity to consciously slow down your heart rate and regulate your breathing. Nervousness is natural, but it can harm our performance by making us rush. A few minutes consciously calming down will be well repaid. There will still be time enough to answer the questions; a strong candidate can answer the 25 questions in less than 45 minutes.

When you do start, go through the whole paper once, identifying the scenarios and questions that look trickiest and marking them for consideration later. When you have skimmed the whole paper turn to one of the scenarios (the first unless it is one that you find particularly difficult) and read it again, this time more slowly and in more detail. Make a few notes to remind you of key aspects of the scenario. Read the scenario a third time. Now turn to the questions associated with that scenario and read through them, mentally ranking them by difficulty. Remember that the scenario may have an elapsed time component so that the questions are effectively sequenced. This does not necessarily mean that you have to answer them in a particular order, but it is likely that answering them in the sequence they are set will trigger your responses more effectively than taking them at random. If you can, try to complete all the questions associated with one scenario before moving on to another, otherwise you will have to spend time later familiarising yourself with the scenario again. If you are really stuck, though, move on so that you do not increase the time pressures. For those you are not sure about, make a note somewhere of the options you are agonising over and jot down your best guess for each.

When you have answered as many of the questions as you can for as many of the scenarios as you can in a first pass you need to decide how to manage a second pass through the paper. Prioritise the remaining questions and scenarios and decide how much time to allocate to each, then work your way through as many of the remaining questions as you can. If the end of the exam looms and your thinking time is almost exhausted go back to your notes on the best guesses for those you have not been able to complete to your full satisfaction and answer with your best guess. There are no penalties for getting things wrong, so it is essential that you select an option for every question, even if it is a random guess.

TAKING THE EXAMINATION

This chapter has, hopefully, armed you for the examination. However, you will know from Foundation or other examinations that you have taken that the perfectly prepared mind can still go blank when you open a real exam paper. If this happens do not despair and, above all, do not panic. Your reaction is a perfectly natural one; your mind is stressed by the challenge ahead and is looking for an opportunity to avoid it.

Here are three strategies to get you going:

- Take a series of deep breaths to ease the panicky feeling and get your pulse back to normal. Raise your head from the desk and think about something else until the feeling of panic subsides. Take a drink of water and something sugary. By the time your brain has had the extra oxygen and sugar it will be ready for action.
- Write something, anything, on a blank piece of paper. Sketch a mind map of some key ideas or make a few notes. This will get your hands moving and connect hand to brain. You may even get real value from what you write down, but the important thing is to get the writing hand moving.
- Read the exam paper and just ignore anything you do not like the look of. You will find a few things that look OK. Get on with these, and pat yourself on the back. You have started.

Time pressure is what causes most people anxiety, yet putting 25 crosses in boxes can be done in less than a minute. Thinking about the answers takes longer, but you will be able to answer the ones you know quite quickly. That will leave plenty of time for the harder ones.

Good luck with your Intermediate Certificate examination.

SUMMARY

In this chapter we have described in some detail how the Intermediate Certificate examination is structured and how best to prepare for it. This should provide the ideal preparation for the examination once you have absorbed the contents of the rest of this book.

Mind maps of the main chapters

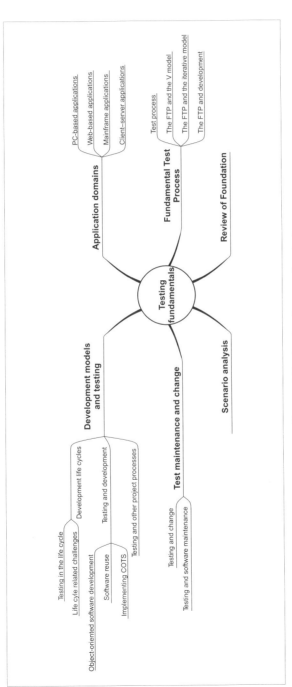

FIGURE A.1   *Chapter 1 Testing fundamentals mind map*

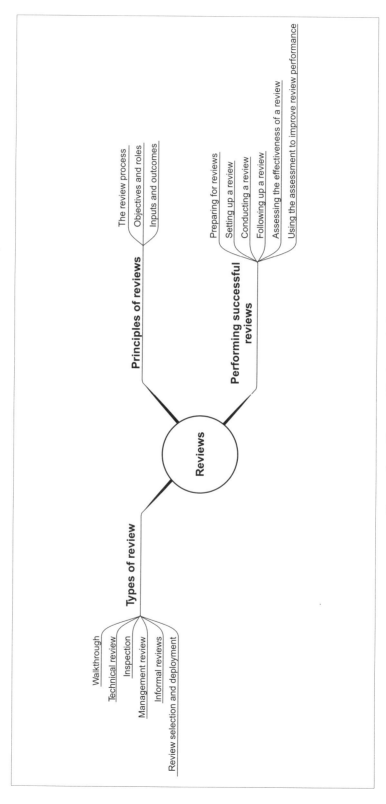

FIGURE A.2 *Chapter 2 Reviews mind map*

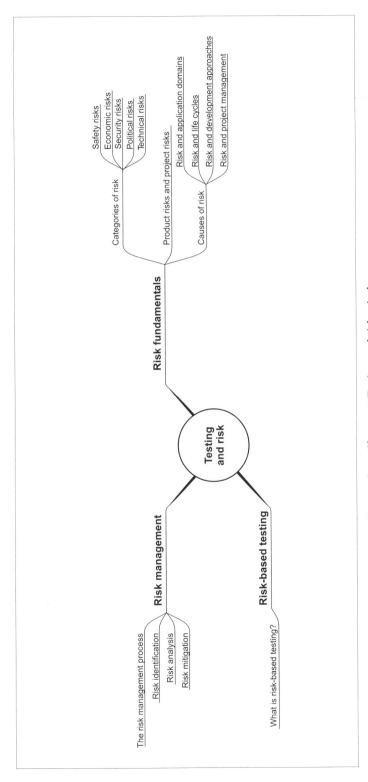

FIGURE A.3   *Chapter 3 Testing and risk mind map*

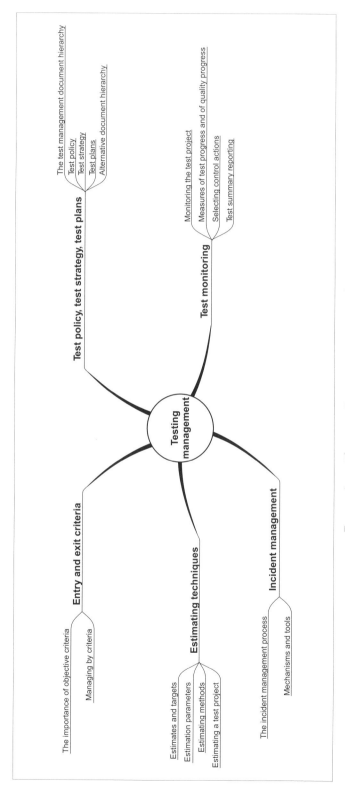

FIGURE A.4   *Chapter 4 Test management mind map*

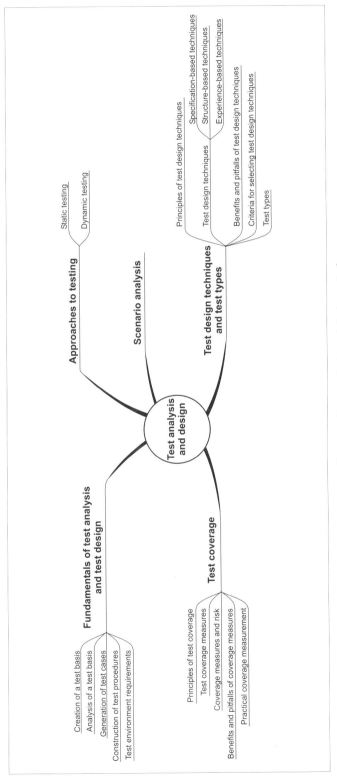

FIGURE A.5   *Chapter 5 Test analysis and design mind map*

Definition, interpretation and examples of K levels

K1 level – knowledge

Definition

Recall appropriate, previously learned information to provide factual answers.

Typical verbs

Recall, select, define, identify.

Examples from testing

Which of the following is the correct definition of . . .?
Select the correct statement about regression testing from . . .
Identify the best reason for testing early from the following . . .

K2 level – comprehension

Definition

Understand the meaning of information and be able to make comparisons.

Typical verbs

Explain, differentiate, summarise, explain.

Examples from testing

Which of the following correctly describes the main difference between regression testing and confirmation testing . . .?
Which of the techniques in list A is most appropriate to each of the applications in list B . . .?

K3 level – application

The K3 level is not used in the Intermediate syllabus or examinations.

K4 level – analysis

Definition

Break down information into parts, examine information and select relevant parts, understand the structure of information.

Typical verbs

Compare, contrast, discriminate, prioritise, relate.

Examples from testing

Which of the test strategy options is most appropriate for the (scenario) project . . .?
Which review technique would be most appropriate for this (scenario) situation?
Which of the actions below should be highest priority at the present (scenario) stage of this (scenario) project . . .?

In these examples (scenario) indicate where information from an associated scenario would determine the appropriate answer.

Higher K levels

Levels K5 (synthesise) and K6 (evaluate) are used in Practitioner level syllabuses and examinations but are not used at the Intermediate level.

Chapter 6 provides further examples of questions at each level.

Index